THE PASTOR & THE PERSONAL COMPUTER

THE PASTOR & THE PERSONAL COMPUTER

Information Management for Ministry

William R. Johnson

Abingdon Press
Nashville

The Pastor and the Personal Computer

Copyright © 1985 by Abingdon Press

All rights reserved
No part of this book may be reproduced in any manner
whatsoever without written permission of the publisher
except brief quotations embodied in critical articles
or reviews. For information address Abingdon Press,
Nashville, Tennessee.

This book is printed on acid-free paper.

Library of Congress Cataloging-in-Publication Data

JOHNSON, WILLIAM R. (WILLIAM RAYMOND), 1951-
The pastor and the personal computer.
1. Pastoral theology—Data processing. 2. Computers.
I. Title
BV4379.U64   1985   253'.028'54   85-9187
ISBN 0-687-30134-3

Scripture quotations are from the Revised Standard Version of the Bible,
copyrighted 1946, 1952, © 1971, 1973 by the Division of Christian
Education of the National Council of Churches of Christ in the U.S.A., and
are used by permission.

The "Glossary of Computer Terms" is from *Selecting The Church Computer*
by William R. Johnson. Copyright © 1984 by Abingdon Press. Used by
permission.

The quotation on page 7, of James Armstrong, is from *Circuit Rider* (p. 11),
vol. 8, no. 9, October 1984. Copyright © 1984 by The United Methodist
Publishing House. Used by Permission.

MANUFACTURED BY THE PARTHENON PRESS AT
NASHVILLE, TENNESSEE, UNITED STATES OF AMERICA

To   Glenn R. Parrott,
pastor extraordinaire,
whose life has shown
the true meaning of discipleship and service,
and whose spirit makes him a saint.

Preface and
Acknowledgments

A pastor is a servant of Christ. This sentence may seem like a strange way to begin a book about computers, yet this book implicitly has more to say about being a pastor than it has to say about computers and computing. It is a resource to assist you in becoming a better pastor through using an amazing technological device—the computer.

James Armstrong, in his article "A Very Personal Word" (*Circuit Rider* magazine, October 1984), states: "The pastoral ministry is the supreme calling of the church, the essential dimension of any other expression of ministry. No office. no ecclesiastical assignment, no defined responsibility within the religious institution can justify or sustain itself apart from other-centered love."

Dr. Armstrong's eloquent and powerful statement about the pastoral ministry touched my heart deeply when I first read it and has infused itself in my spirit as I consider the nature and reasons for my ministry. God called me to the pastoral ministry long before I realized the validity of the call. When the call became clear and I finally accepted it, my career as a computer professional was already under way. Yet, in a move few people understood, I left the computer world to enter Christ's universe as a pastor. My time as a parish priest in two United Methodist charges were privileges that taught me the meaning of the words *joy, humility, compassion,* and *grace.* Indeed, by the grace of God, I believe I learned more from those congregations in five years than I could have ever taught them in fifty. My heart has always been in the work of a parish priest and will always remain there in whatever God calls ɪne to do in his magnificent church.

It is from the depths of my pastoral experience and from my heart that I have striven to write this book from a pastor's viewpoint. In other words, I understand the joys and the sorrows, the wonder and the frustration, the happiness and the pain of being a pastor. I understand the mysterious calling to ministry that makes being a pastor more than a vocation. That is why this is a book about pastors—for pastors ministering in the information age.

This book will not discuss every possible way in which a computer can be used in the pastoral ministry. Rather, it is designed to open up new doors for you in managing ministry information. It is intended to help you move confidently into the information age and become a more humble, gracious servant of Christ. It is my hope that this volume will help you to see and know that "the pastoral ministry is the supreme calling of the church."

There are many persons to whom I am eternally grateful for their guidance and suggestions during the writing of *The Pastor and the Personal Computer Book*.

ANN JOHNSON—my wife and most intimate earthly friend whose love is never ending and whose face never fails to brighten the room with the light of Christ; for typing, reading, suggesting, and supporting as the manuscript was written and edited.

ALBERT E. FIFHAUSE—friend, pastor, and associate whose gifts of creativity and grace are precious assets to the church of Christ; for reading and reacting to the manuscript in its early days.

KAYO SUZUKIDA—friend and secretary whose patience and understanding never ceased to amaze me; for reading and reacting to the manuscript.

BISHOP EDWIN C. BOULTON—friend and diocesan vicar of the Dakotas whose grace, compassion, and episcopal leadership are filled with such power that Christ is always served; for writing the foreword.

BISHOP JAMES S. THOMAS—friend and bishop whose humility, empathy, and love never show the man but always show God and cause people around him to know they have been in the presence of a true saint; for writing the foreword.

The congregations of Greeley United Methodist Church, Greeley, Iowa; St. Paul's United Methodist Church, Waukon, Iowa; and St. John's United Methodist Church, Dorchester, Iowa—whose patience and beauty enabled me, a naive, young man, to learn the meaning of the word *pastor* and who will always be in my heart and spirit forever.

To all these and many others, I am humbly thankful.

Bill (William R. Johnson)
December, 1984

Contents

List of Figures

Foreword

There are few technologies that have impacted the current scene any more than the computer. Without the computer, space flight would be all but impossible, and at the pedestrian level of grocery shopping, few of us purchase a can of tomatoes without the computer registering the purchase in an inventory control program.

The church, too, is becoming increasingly conscious of new possibilities for the use of the computer in its overall program. We celebrate that fact and are thankful that one of the persons with exceptional expertise in the area is William R. Johnson, a United Methodist pastor. While Dr. Johnson has served on the staff of the General Council on Finance and Administration of The United Methodist Church, his innovative leadership in computer technology has been used nationally in The United Methodist Church. His first book, *Selecting the Church Computer*, focuses on the possibilities of computer technology at the local church and judicatory levels.

We are pleased to submit the foreword to this, his second book, which is designed to help pastors understand how the computer can be of value in pastoral ministry.

Prior to accepting his positions with the judicatory bodies of the national chuch, Bill served effectively as a local church pastor. We both knew him as a parish priest, and rejoice that he has a deep sensitivity for persons and for the local parish. One of the inherent dangers in any technology is its potentially dehumanizing influence. Social Security numbers and keypunch cards may identify us as digits in a vastly impersonal catalogue, but that is all they do. In a somewhat depersonalizing science, we believe Bill brings a high technological skill laced with a sensitivity for persons and a solid understanding of the local church, all of which will make his contribution to the field highly significant.

Sociologists refer to our time as the information age. A question that must be answered by all of us, and most certainly by every busy pastor, is whether the spate of data available to us will be ignored or will be put to constructive use. Dr. Johnson effectively addresses these issues, and suggests ways in which the computer, an increasingly cost-effective tool, can be put to transforming use in the information age. The computer is not a toy. Nor will it be a magic potion for the unmotivated. It can be a constructive tool for the pastor and local church where there is a desire to manage information for ministry.

The primary benefit of a computer wisely matched to the needs of a local church is in time released from organizational, study, and administrative detail. Interestingly, a piece of hardware, a complex technology well applied, has the potential of creating performance patterns for pastor and staff, which will enhance their ability to be more humane and caring.

Chapters 9 through 12 suggest possible ways to implement this new technology, ranging through membership data, administrative procedures, financial management, and worship applications.

It is a temptation to elaborate here on what Dr. Johnson so appropriately focuses on in chapter 13. Clergy are as subject to fads as anyone. Because there is nothing magical in what a computer can do, it will never be more than a tool that, when appropriately applied to the total task of ministry, can enhance our use of time. The great gifts of sensitivity, devotion to God, love for people, creativity and imagination, and the ability to dream dreams and see visions will never be replaced by a manual we read nor by a machine plugged into an electrical outlet.

We are thankful that a pastor who has clearly demonstrated the gifts of God's Spirit in his own ministry can show us some of the ways to magnify those gifts through the application of a fascinating new technology.

Bishop James S. Thomas
  Ohio East Area of The
  United Methodist Church
  and 1984-85 President of the
  Council of Bishops of
  The United Methodist Church

Bishop Edwin C. Boulton
  Dakotas Area of The
  United Methodist Church

SECTION 1

INTRODUCTION

1

The Pastor in the Information Age

But as for you . . . aim at righteousness, godliness, faith, love, steadfastness, gentleness.

I Timothy 6:11

A pastor is a person of unique abilities and special gifts, divinely called to serve the people of God. A pastor* engages in a sacramental ministry as a servant of Christ directed toward the people of God, usually in the context of a local congregation. While the pastor is a minister in the sense of performing ministry, the pastor is also uniquely a shepherd—a person who tends the flock and feeds the sheep of Christ.

In a world where information continues to have an increasingly important role in daily decisions, the effectiveness of a church's ministry is directly dependent upon the constant flow of accurate and useful information. Most of the information management in a local church is the pastor's responsibility as he or she guides and leads the congregation.

_____

*I prefer the title "pastor" rather than "minister" because, in my opinion, the word *minister* is more a verb than a noun. To minister is to serve. To be a minister of Word, order, and sacrament is to be a pastor. The book of Hebrews discusses the priesthood of all believers, and in presenting this concept, the writer of Hebrews communicates that all who believe in the saving grace of Jesus Christ are ministers of his Word. Regardless of lay or ordained status, *all Christians* minister to one another and to the rest of the world as the unified Body of Christ. Thus, the word *pastor* is a part of the larger meaning contained in the word *minister*. Any tools which assist a pastor in serving the Body of Christ and leading a congregation's ministry are merely means to the end. This book proposes to discuss how one of those modern tools, the computer, can assist the pastor in becoming a more effective servant of Christ in an information rich, technologically dependent society.

The Pastoral Ministry

The work of a pastor has existed for thousands of years. Old Testament and other ancient writings bear a historical witness that many persons of special gifts and graces were divinely called to serve as rabbis and priests in a variety of contexts. God called them to his service, and they responded to that call in faithfulness. Indeed, throughout history it is clear that God has called and appointed persons from all stations of life to serve as religious leaders.

The unique context of being a Christian pastor began some two thousand years ago when Christ sent the twelve apostles into the towns and villages to preach the Word, heal the sick, and witness God's liberating grace. Up until the twentieth century, pastors were generally itinerant, moving from town to town on foot and horseback, occasionally establishing lay preaching points for the edification of believers. In the twentieth century, however, the itinerant nature of pastoral ministry has substantially diminished with a pastor serving a local congregation for several years. Pastorates of several years have transformed the historic context of ministry from those first days in Palestine as society and culture has changed. However, the common thread between past and present pastoral ministry is the call of Jesus Christ, God Incarnate. The pastor is a person God has called to be a shepherd of Christ who tends the flock in many ways.

The typical twentieth-century pastor ministers to a local congregation that is relatively stable and has been established in the community for fifty to two hundred years. He or she places roots in a community by joining community groups, sending children to the local schools, and voting in local elections. Generally, pastors serve in the same community for several years, with pastorates of eight to twelve years becoming increasingly common. Ministry of this sort requires the pastor to constantly develop and change his or her ideas and information about the community and congregation. Being a shepherd requires special gifts and graces which God provides to those whom he calls. To be an effective pastor in the information age is a difficult task that uses God's gifts and graces to the fullest extent possible.* Pastoral ministry requires great risks and the ability to summon God's grace in the most tenuous of moments. A pastor must have empathy, sensitivity, grace, caring, compassion, forgiveness, love, understanding, humility, fairness, and other qualities which the world respects, but does not highly prize on the road to success. Information age ministry also requires a pastor to have a broad background. This background should be sufficient so a pastor can be a generalist in many areas, and yet, a specialist in others. At the same time, a pastor must be a better than average communicator in order to share the gospel of Christ. A modern pastor must also be an administrator, organizer, and controller of information. These skills and gifts, by their very nature, are conflicting and paradoxical. Thus, the plight of a local church pastor is often difficult and lonely while interspersed with periods of joy and great satisfaction.

———

*The term "information age" in this book refers to that period of history in which informed and effective decisions on either a societal or individual level are highly dependent upon accurate, reliable, and useful information. I believe humanity is presently traversing through the information age.

Ministry Information Management

As previously discussed, pastoring has existed for at least two millennia with its roots preceding Christ by thousands of years. Yet, even though working electronic computers have only existed since the early 1940's, the ability of computers to efficiently organize information in beneficial ways can be used in pastoral ministry.

The knowledge a pastor needs for effective ministry ranges from the general to the specific. Many kinds of information must be received, processed, and used in the pastoral ministry. Ways to efficiently manage ministry information are needed to help a pastor in serving his or her church.

Pastoral information can be gleaned from many sources. Some of these sources include church records, parishioners, books, theological journals, data from national and regional judicatory church bodies, local community information, news from local media, and congregational gossip. The information itself can be anything from a simple statement of fact to a lengthy opinion. Some information is useful while other information may be discarded. In addition, some information may not be valuable immediately, but may be of enormous benefit in the future. In any case, information that benefits pastoral work appears in both predictable and unpredictable ways, taking expected and unexpected forms.

The information a pastor needs can be simple or complex in its raw state or in its ultimate application. Regardless of the nature, type, or source of the information, it must be organized, managed, and administered. Without organization, information is of little value or use. For example, it makes little sense to place a news item about a church activity in the church's master membership records. This is an absurd example, but illustrates that information in the pastoral ministry must be organized in order to increase pastoral effectiveness.

The organization, management, and administration of information for the ministry is time consuming and tedious for most pastors. The majority of pastors feel that they did not attend seminary or Bible college to become administrators. Indeed, many pastors claim they do not have or want a gift for administration. Yet, pastor after pastor has very quickly discovered that survival within the church requires him or her to be an administrator. Hence, pastors are forced to develop administrative skills in organizing information to increase and maintain effectiveness.

Most information age pastors use manual systems for maintaining information, which includes paper and pencils, notebooks and file folders, typewriters and copy machines, and other similar tools. Such a manual system frequently requires many hours of analyzing the available information and classifying it into proper categories so it can be effectively used. In addition, information management requires a pastor to become skilled in office management procedures such as filing and typing.

The Paradox of Ministry Information Management

Developing information management skills usually means that you spend less time with church members because you are trying to manage information. Thus, the paradox of ministry information management strikes like a bolt of lightning. You must apply the information so that your ministry may be more effective. Yet, your ministry may become less effective because you have to spend too much time administering your information! Information age pastors are often faced with this confusing and frustrating paradoxical dilemma.

Information Management Tools

Relieving or even removing the paradox of ministry information management requires effective tools. Some of these tools include typewriters, duplicating machines (mimeo, photographic, etc.), pencils, paper clips, staples, scissors, tape, paste, and a host of other items. It is quite likely that you are familiar with most common information management tools and have used several of them for various reasons.

The purpose of these tools is to assist you, as a pastor, in the management of information by (1) efficiently organizing and maintaining available information, and (2) reducing the ministry information management paradox. In other words, the different tools that benefit persons in the business of information management can also greatly benefit you as a pastor.

No tool by itself can completely eliminate the ministry information management paradox. In fact, any one of the tools (if not used properly) can make it worse! It is only through an effective combination of all tools that the paradox finally meets its match.

Up to this point, you probably have not given the tools used to manage your information a second thought. Yet, these tools should not be taken for granted. Without them, much of what you are able to accomplish as a pastor would not be possible and your pastoral ministry would be rendered ineffective.

Try to imagine a church without a duplicating machine. It would be extremely difficult to create a proper Sunday bulletin or publish a monthly newsletter. Indeed, without a duplicating machine of some kind, you probably would throw up your hands and say that the value of the bulletin and the monthly newsletter is questionable. Why bother to publish a bulletin or newsletter if the proper mechanisms don't exist to produce it? Without the tools to achieve your work, the value of the work suddenly diminishes.

However, when technology (such as a mimeograph machine) is introduced, new ways to express your work are suddenly discovered and your church's ministry is strengthened as a result. Because the mimeograph makes something possible that was impossible before, it saves time in ways that were not previously imagined. It helps you to achieve the purpose of your calling: the mission of Jesus Christ and the ministry of the servant pastor.

The Computer: Tool of Information Management

Many modern technological tools exist for the management of information. These tools have been used efficiently in both profit and nonprofit organizations, resulting in incredibly effective products and work. The church is also beginning to realize the extensive value of such modern technological tools. As the church searches for new methods of ministry in a technological society, more of the new technology comes into the church every day.

One of the new technological tools of information management is the computer. In fact, *the* tool of information management now and in the future is the computer. The computer is here to stay, and like the duplicating machine in a local church, imaginations are hard pressed to dream of an information-rich society without the aid of computers. The computer is also an electronic device that can enormously assist pastors in practical ministry. As a typical pastor, you are serving one or more churches with between one hundred and seven hundred members. You may be fortunate enough to have a part-time or even full-time secretary. However, it is also true that pastors of the smallest churches must do almost all of the church's "administrivia" themselves. (Administrivia consists of those tasks required to classify, process, and maintain the minute details of information. Those tasks include typing, filing, organizing, etc.) As a tool, the computer can be of inestimable value in the information needs and requirements of a pastor. Greater efficiency in ministry information management can lead to increased pastoral effectiveness by reducing or completely eliminating the information management paradox.

An Assumption

One of the basic assumptions of this book and of information management is that the computer is a tool. The computer is not a panacea, nor is it the miracle machine that most vendors claim, nor is it the saving grace from all you do as a pastor. It is a tool. Computers cannot be more and they cannot be less than information management tools.

Computers should not be used just because computers exist. Just because a mountain is there doesn't mean you have to climb it. If you cannot identify ways in which a computer will benefit your ministry, then you should not use it. When a computer has no identifiable benefits for your pastoral ministry, it will probably frustrate you and raise your anxiety level, thereby aggravating the ministry information management paradox.

The tool perspective is vitally important when discussing computers. Computers are tools like typewriters or mimeograph machines; they are designed to help manage information more efficiently so that ministry becomes more effective. The computer is not an end in itself but a means to the end. It is a means for ministry information management so that you, as a pastor, can become an increasingly effective servant and disciple of Christ.

SECTION 2

THE WORLD OF COMPUTERS

2

What Good Is It?

And God saw everything that he had made, and behold, it was very good.

Genesis 1:31

When you consider purchasing something, it is natural to wonder what good can possibly come from it. In other words, what good is it? In most circumstances, a need precipitates the item's acquisition. For example, if you need to keep a gallon of milk cold, a refrigerator is required. If you want to wash your clothes efficiently, a washing machine is necessary. Most folks do not acquire an item unless it provides some identifiable benefit.

In the same way that you consider household purchases, you should know how a computer can help you. However, identifying the benefits of a computer is more nebulous and complicated than knowing a refrigerator keeps food cold or a washing machine cleans clothes. Yet, even though it's difficult to ascertain a computer's usefulness for the pastoral ministry, the need to know about its value is not diminished. The result is a logical contradiction that has you wondering what the true value of a computer really is, yet feeling like you have to obtain one first to discover the machine's benefits for ministry. In other words, what comes first: the chicken or the egg?

When any person or organization desires to use a computer in their work, understanding the computer's benefits is vitally important. This knowledge will keep the user using the computer as a tool rather than allowing the machine to become the end in itself.

Quantitative and Qualitative Benefits

The benefits of a computer can be placed in quantitative and qualitative categories. A quantitative benefit is measurable and demonstrable. A quantitative benefit is when because X was done, Y was achieved. For example, if a computer permits completion of a project in two hours when that project used to take five hours with manual systems, then a quantitative benefit has been achieved. In other words, through the use of a computer, the project's completion time has been reduced from five hours to two hours resulting in a quantifiable, measurable savings of three hours.

On the other hand, some benefits of a computer may not be quantitative. Nonmeasurable benefits are generally related to the improved quality of work rather than the quantity of work achieved. For example, if a computer helps you respond more quickly with vital information to a crisis situation in your parish, then the quality of ministry may be perceived as being improved even though the quantity of work may not have changed. A qualitative benefit from a computer is subjective in determination whereas a quantitative benefit is an objective determination.

If possible, both quantitative (measurable) and qualitative (nonmeasurable) benefits of a computer in pastoral ministry should be identified. This knowledge will then help you to be more keenly aware of the computer's end benefit: increased ministry effectiveness in the name of Jesus Christ.

Selecting the Right Computer:
Needs and Benefits

The process of selecting a computer for your work is not complicated if you begin at the right place. The selective process can, however, be confusing if you do not give it the careful thought it warrants. The computer selection process begins with identifying your needs and then understanding the benefits of the computer when the needs are met.

You do not have to become a computer professional, a highly educated computer hobbyist, or a computer science theorist to use a computer in your work. Most of the smaller computers in today's marketplace, often called microcomputers, will support your work. However, you do need to become familiar with your pastoral ministry information needs and benefits, some computer terms, and certain administrative and operational procedures needed to use a computer.

Consumers are bombarded with a myriad of screaming computer advertisements, announcing the panacea of panaceas that claims to solve all your problems with the push of a single button. But don't let the advertisements lull you into a false sense of security or intimidate you with technical jargon. Above all, don't believe everything you read in the ads. They make computers sound so simple, yet those who use computers at the professional level know that simplicity is not a virtue of those marvelous machines. In fact, the computer industry doesn't have the words *simple* or *simplicity* in its vocabulary. However, you can be assured that computer advertisements are attempting to lure you into the store to view, touch, and drool over the assorted buffet of computer goodies. These goodies consist of a variety of computers sitting on tables and desks with some spectacular demonstration of multicolor graphics on their screens.

If the advertisement does lead you into a computer store, you are usually immediately accosted by one or two sales representatives who want to know what you are interested in and how they can help. No matter what your initial response may be, you will be told they have exactly what you need to solve your problems. It's amazing that a computer salesperson knows precisely what will solve your ministry information problems from a simple statement you have made! Like any sales pitch, computer vendors approach you with certain preconceived notions about how you think and what it is you need and want. They use certain emotional tactics to draw you away from what your original desires might be in order to discuss a more expensive machine. It is no secret that computer sales representatives have attended the same sales schools, read the same sales concepts, and use the same techniques that car, appliance, and real estate salespeople use. They are highly motivated by one word: *commission.*

Do *not* begin your computer selection process by looking at the computer hardware. ("Hardware" is a computer term used to define the physical, tangible pieces of equipment.) Never, never choose the computer hardware before understanding what your needs are and whether the benefits of a computer justifies its acquisition. In fairness to computer salespeople, I realize that they have to make a living just like everyone else, and most are honest, well-meaning individuals. However, if you start selecting a computer by examining hardware and talking with salespeople, a mistake can be made that you will live to regret: the purchase of an expensive, impractical toy rather than a professional tool for ministry.

The Needs Analysis

The first step in selecting a computer for the pastoral ministry is to decide exactly what it is you intend to do with a computer. This is called a *needs analysis* in the computer industry. An information needs analysis in pastoral ministry attempts to scrutinize and study precisely what your current ministry information management needs are.

A needs analysis is not necessarily complicated nor does it need to be complex. Many methodologies exist to accomplish a needs analysis. Some of these methods are good, and some are not. You may wish to research some of these methods, or it may be better for you to design your own methodology. I discovered in my pastoral ministry that every pastor has a unique style of ministry and knows how he or she works. Therefore, complex needs analysis methodologies found in other books will probably not be of much value other than in helping you think about how a needs analysis is done. Some general guidelines and comments are offered in the following paragraphs that will help you identify your needs.

A needs analysis attempts to account for the tasks you complete through manual systems. It identifies how you receive information, the sources of your information, how the information is processed, and how the processed information is used in ministry.

An example may be helpful. Most pastors publish a monthly or weekly church newsletter. Church newsletters have many different forms and are completed in a variety of ways depending upon the church's need. The newsletter generally contains news stories about past and upcoming events in the parish, personal items about parishioners (e.g., graduations, marriages, illnesses), devotional writings, and filler items such as jokes or poems. The church newsletter is a communications tool that requires the gathering, processing, and dissemination of information in a published format.

To create the newsletter, you as pastor, your secretary (if you have one!), and others will receive news from parishioners and many other sources about current events. If you use a manual system, you might write a piece of information on a scrap of paper, tear it out of the local newspaper, or make a mental note of it. You might place that information in a file folder or mental file to be used in the next newsletter. When the deadline arrives for publishing the next newsletter, you would get your raw information file in whatever form it is kept and process the data into a publishable format. The processing consists of writing, editing, and organizing the information into your church's newsletter. The processing continues until the finished product is completed by typing, duplicating, addressing, and mailing. The church newsletter follows an information processing system where data is received, processed, distributed, and used for the church's benefit.

Whether you handle every newsletter detail or serve as publisher while others complete the details, the monthly newsletter example is a simple description of one small facet in the pastoral ministry. A needs analysis of your ministry takes into account the sources of newsletter information, how that information is maintained in files, how it is processed, and how the end product is distributed and used. In general, a needs analysis methodically determines the various tasks that you complete in your daily work as a pastor. *Any pastoral activity* that uses information should be part of your ministry information needs analysis.

To begin your needs analysis process, write down the tasks to be analyzed. Then list the following items for each task:

Gathering data and from what sources
Maintenance, e.g., paper in file folders
Processing
Distribution, e.g., to your church members or for personal use
Use

The information gathered in the need analysis should be organized so that it parallels your administrative style of pastoral ministry. It will take days to complete the needs analysis. Information in other sections of this book may help you with completing the analysis. Detailed discussions of practical computer applications for the pastoral ministry can be found in chapters 9 through 12. In addition, Appendix 1 contains an applications index with brief descriptions of the possible pastoral computer uses.

Benefits

The second step in selecting a computer is to identify the potential benefits a computer may have for your pastoral ministry. In other words, can you justify the purchase of a computer in your ministry? You should be able to clearly demonstrate to your personal satisfaction that a computer will provide direct quantitative and qualitative benefits for you. Since you have to decide about buying a computer, you must satisfy yourself that the computer will help you. If you cannot assure yourself that a computer will help, then don't put yourself through the frustration of trying to make a machine do something it can't.

The following example may clarify the benefits of a computer in pastoral ministry. As a pastor, your needs analysis may show that you recognize the birthdays of church members. In a manual system, a handwritten or typed birthday list file must be maintained. Perhaps once each week or month, you remove these birthday lists from your filing cabinet and make the appropriate response. The response might be a telephone call, birthday card, or pastoral visit. Using a manual system, this process can be time-consuming and tedious, taking between thirty minutes and five hours a month depending upon the size of your congregation.

Using a computer in birthday recognition will save time, resulting in a quantitative benefit. If the church members' names are loaded into the computer with their birthdates, the machine can generate a list of birthdays in any specified week or month. At the same time that the computer produces the list, it can also print the address, telephone number, and other relevant information for the church member on that list. The computer may take five minutes or less to produce such a birthday list or directory. Therefore, a quantitative benefit has been received. The time needed to produce a birthday list has been reduced from thirty to five minutes. The additional twenty-five minutes can be used to make several telephone calls to the birthday persons or for other things. Saved time also gives an indirect qualitative benefit, which frees you to complete more pressing tasks directly related to ministry.

It is not necessary to spend a large amount of time justifying a computer for your ministry. Identifying the quantitative and qualitative benefits of a computer system should not be difficult if your needs analysis has been carefully and thoroughly completed. On the other hand, you should spend enough time identifying benefits to convince yourself that a computer will help in your ministry. Once you are convinced, then you are ready to proceed with the next two steps of computer selection: software and hardware.

Software Selection

Now you are prepared to move into the third phase of selecting a pastoral computer: software comparison, evaluation, and selection. *Software* is a term for computer programs. Software is what makes the machine function. It tells the computer exactly what to do and when to do it.

There are many varieties of software that will help your pastoral work. Choosing the right software is a relatively subjective process. Armed with your needs analysis, you determine what software comes closest to meeting your needs. There is probably no software that will meet your needs exactly, so you must make a decision about which software will work the best for you. The factors to consider in software selection are discussed in chapter 4.

Hardware Selection

The fourth phase in choosing a computer is hardware evaluation and selection. (Hardware refers to the tangible pieces of the computer.) This phase can be complicated, but it is also the most objective part of the selection process. The hardware decision really comes quite naturally if you have faithfully identified needs, determined benefits, and selected the right software. Hardware selection is discussed in chapter 5.

As you can see, selecting a pastoral computer does not begin by walking into a computer store and examining the wares. As wonderful and glamorous as the machines may appear in the store, you can be severely misled as the sales representative guides you through a preprogrammed demonstration. First, start with your needs. Then, determine the benefits. Follow that by choosing the software, and finally, select the hardware.

Reasons Not to Buy a Computer

It's true—computers *are* fun. They are surrounded with a great deal of glitter, glamour, and attractiveness. However, fun and attractiveness are not valid reasons or benefits for having a computer in pastoral ministry. As the church computer market has demonstrated, there are some people who become so enamored by the fun aspects of the computer that the real tasks of ministry are ignored. The hobby should not replace the profession. While using a computer system may indeed be fun, the benefits of a computer for ministry are serious and should produce an improved ministry.

The computer is a tool, and pastors who use it for ministry should view its benefits with professional respect. If you purchase a computer to play games, then expect to have fun. If you purchase a computer to assist with your ministry, then expect to serve Christ in more meaningful ways.

The Primary Benefit

What is the primary benefit of a computer for you? What good is it? Basically, the primary benefit of a pastoral computer is the time saved from organizational administrivia, which produces a qualitatively improved ministry. Because the time saved creates more opportunities for pastoral ministry on a human level, it releases you for contact with church members. A computer allows you to fulfill the role of shepherd more effectively. It allows a pastor to have more time to give his or her congregation a word of hope, a word of compassion, a word of grace, and a word of Jesus Christ.

While the primary benefit of computers in pastoral ministry is noble and serves Christ, it has a worldly reality: it will cost money. You have to decide if the benefits are worth the several thousand dollars you or your church will have to invest in a computer. If you purchase a computer, do not expect to save money. You will not enjoy a monetary profit. You will not have a new material possession other than the machine itself. What you will have is time saved, creating a more efficient way to organize and manage information and resulting in a more effective pastoral ministry. If you cannot justify the primary benefit of a computer for your pastoral work, then you should not use one.

What good is it? A computer is good when it helps a pastor become a better pastor through both quantitative and qualitative benefits. It is not good if it creates convenient excuses for a pastor not to do the work of ministry while playing electronic games or writing computer programs. The computer is a tool. It is a tool that can provide tremendous benefits when used appropriately.

3

A Computer Primer

It is good for me that I was afflicted, that I might learn thy statutes.

Psalm 119:71

The computer is generally misunderstood by most people. It's somewhat of a paradox that people think users have to be mathematical geniuses to use a computer and yet, somehow, the machine thinks by itself.

The computer is a modern technological tool that does not require in-depth mathematical knowledge and, contrary to popular belief, the computer does not think for itself. As a pastor, you are called to be a servant of Christ and a shepherd of his flock. You are not expected to be a mathematical wizard or computer professional in the pastoral ministry. The technical details and programming of a computer should be left to professionals trained in the computer sciences. However, in using a computer, perserverance and patience are required. Without these qualities, a computer may never help you become a more effective pastor or give you additional time to work with church members.

Learning to use a computer is similar to using a typewriter. In order to use a typewriter, a person has to become familiar with the particular machine available to him or her. After a period of time, the idiosyncracies of that typewriter become apparent and its general usefulness for administrative work becomes obvious. This increasing familiarity requires a certain level of knowledge about the typewriter keys and buttons. You learn which buttons accomplish which actions. However, that knowledge does not include mechanical information about how the typewriter works internally. You do not have to become familiar with the detailed operation of a hammer when a key is pressed in order to use the typewriter. However, you do have to know how to set margins, use the tab key, and when to press the shift key for capital letters.

Like the typewriter, a certain level of knowledge is required to use a computer. You need to know what buttons to press, and when to press them in order to accomplish desired actions. However, like the typewriter, you do not need to know how the action is completed. You only need to know that it is done when the proper sequence of keys is pressed. Thus, familiarity with the machine and its usefulness is required on the "what" and "when" level, but not on the "how" level. To use the computer, you simply need to know what commands to enter in order to produce the desired results. Detailed knowledge about the internal transformation of data and electronic workings of the computer are not necessary.

A brief and simple description of the what, when, and how concerning computers follows. This description is not intended to provide detailed technical knowledge about computers, but to help you gain an elementary understanding of how computers function internally. Hopefully, this narrative will reduce some of the mystery behind the machine and help you to see its usefulness as a tool.

Computer Circuits

A computer is a relatively complex device that functions in a relatively simple way. Any computer is a machine composed of thousands of electronic circuits and wires. These circuits are designed to carry electrical impulses or messages that are basically in one of two states: "on" or "off." Computer circuits function much like a light bulb that can be turned on and off from a wall switch. Information typed into a computer is transformed into the on and off states of the machine's electronic circuits. When the computer prints something on its screen or printer, the information is transformed from the electronic on and off states to a visual record in letters, numbers, and punctuation that human beings understand. The transformation process between machine readable electronic impulses (on and off) and humanly readable visual images is invisible to the user. You do not know it is happening nor do you need to know how the transformation works.

Computer Super Highways

When information needs to be transferred from one area to another in the machine, it travels on electronic "super highways." These super highways have entrances and exits that allow information to travel to and from certain points accomplishing specified tasks. When you push the key labeled "A" on the keyboard, an electronic code (with on and off signals) is generated representing the letter "A" in the computer. This code then enters the super highway traveling to the major intersection where all the highways meet. Here the code exits from the super highway and stops for a traffic officer to direct it to the next destination. Once the traffic officer has determined where the "A" wants to go, the traffic officer blows a whistle and directs it back onto the super highway towards its destination. At the destination, the "A" leaves the super highway, parks along the road, and completes any required action. After this, the "A" may also be directed back onto another super highway to another part of the computer, depending upon the operator's original intentions.

To accomplish the simplified process just described, a series of programmed electronic circuits and mechanical components must work in harmony with one another. If these parts fail to work together or if the programming is incorrect when the key "A" is pressed, the information may not enter the proper place on the super highway nor exit at the proper destination, which causes unpredictable results. In other words, "accidents" and "snowstorms" occasionally occur on the computer's super highway, which causes delays or even complete disruption of information movement in the computer.

I have just described how a computer works without becoming technical. As you can imagine, volumes and volumes of material have been written on the technical aspects of computers. If you are interested in a more academic approach about how a computer functions, I suggest that you check the computer science section of a local university, college, or public library for a book that describes the technical functions of the super highway.

Computer Classifications

Working computers have existed since the early 1940s. The first computers were used in military applications expanding from there into the business realm. The first computers were also large in a physical sense and, in some instances, larger in memory and storage capacity than certain present-day computers. However, the late 1970s and early 1980s brought the development of much smaller computers in price ranges that allowed average consumers to buy one. In other words, the computer industry existed for almost three and one-half decades before the personal computer market opened up.

The home computer market spawned a group of people called computer hobbyists that have no training in the computer sciences, but claim knowledge of all computer aspects. Unfortunately, the computer hobbyist attitude has confused the computer market with claims that whatever tasks the large computers can do, microcomputers can do better and less expensively. Most of these claims are wrong and based on insufficient knowledge of larger computers.

To help you sort out the claims and counterclaims in the hobbyist versus professional computer wars, the following three main computer size classifications and their subclassifications are defined.

Mainframe

Mainframe computers are very large machines that can support literally hundreds and even thousands of terminals at one time. (A terminal is a device that communicates with a computer. Terminals usually look like televisions with keyboards.) Mainframe computers can do a great many tasks at one time and are used by airlines, oil companies, national governments, and other large organizations. Mainframe computers cost between half-a-million and twenty million dollars. The sale of mainframe computers account for more than 50 percent of computer industry revenues.

Mainframes are subclassed into two categories:
— Super-computers. These are the largest computers in existence. They cost in excess of five million dollars for just one computer.
— Regular mainframes. These are the mainstays of the computer industry.

Mini-computers

Mini-computers are large machines that can usually support between twenty and one hundred fifty terminals at any one time. Mini-computers, like mainframes, are multi-task devices. Multi-task means that many tasks can be processed at one time by the computer. In other words, while a set of labels is printing, an operator can be doing word processing and someone else can print a financial report at the same time. Mini-computers are used in large, medium, and small businesses. This type of computer typically costs between forty thousand and one and one-half million dollars.

Mini-computers can be subclassed into three categories:
— Super-minis. Some professionals say that super-minis are really small mainframes.
— Medium minis. This is the most common size of mini-computer in the business world.
— Low-end minis. This group consists of smaller computers that approach the micro-computer range.

Micro-computers

Micro-computers are the most recent marketplace entries of the computer industry. Unlike mainframes and mini-computers, micro-computers are single-task machines, which means they can only do one task at a time. When a micro-computer is printing labels, it must be dedicated to that task. The machine cannot be used for anything else until the labels are finished. Hence, a micro-computer is often dubbed personal because it can do only one task at a time for one person. Micro-computers are found in homes and businesses of all sizes, and are used for a number of purposes. This size computer is the most appropriate and most realistic computer for the pastoral ministry. Micro-computers cost between five hundred and thirty thousand dollars.

Micro-computers are subclassed into three categories:

— Super-micros. Some professionals say that super-micros are really low-end minis.
— Professional. This group of machines is used primarily by business and computer professionals.
— Home. This group of micro-computers is used by home consumers and hobbyists.

Some Computer Terms

As you move toward using a computer in your ministry, some definitions of computer terms are necessary. These terms are not difficult to understand or use; however, without them you can be lost in a computer conversation or while reading manuals and/or articles about computers.

The following terms provide enough information so you can carry on an intelligent conversation with another person about computers and continue to read this book with understanding. The terms are defined in everyday language and attempt to avoid technical definitions.

Appendix 2 is a more lengthy glossary of computer terms that are relatively common in the computer world. You may wish to consult it from time to time when you encounter an unfamiliar term. For an even more comprehensive glossary of computer terms, other books are available, and you may wish to obtain one for your library.

Bit	—The smallest unit of storage in a computer; a bit must always equal 0 or 1.
Byte	—A unit of storage; one byte equals one character where a character is a letter, number, punctuation or the blank space; one byte usually equals 8 bits.
CPU	—Central Processing Unit: the computer's traffic officer that directs all functions of the machine; synonym is *processor*.
Disk	—A form of magnetic storage media capable of storing millions of characters; floppy disks and hard disks are the most common.
K	—Kilobyte; a unit of storage; 1K equals 1,024 bytes; normally shortened to mean 1,000 bytes, e.g., 128K usually means 128,-000 bytes; usually refers to processor memory.
MB	—Megabyte; a unit of storage, 1MB equals 1,000,000 bytes; usually refers to the capacity of a disk.
Modem	—A communications device that allows two computers to "talk" over a telephone line.
Interface	—A standard or convention that permits two pieces of computer hardware to be connected with one another.
Monitor	—A television-like screen that presents information in a form readable by human beings.
Operating System (OS)	—Software in the CPU that directs the computer in all of its functions; common OS's include CP/M, MS-DOS, and Unix.

4

The Question of Software

Train yourself in godliness; for while bodily training is of some value, godliness is of value in every way, as it holds promise for the present life and also for the life to come.
I Timothy 4:7b-8

Computers are similar in concept to the wholeness of a human being. Computer hardware is like the physical body of a human being. Computer software is much like the human spirit. The spirit enables the body to function and gives the body its personality. During a normal earthly existence, the body and spirit are inseparable. In computers, the software gives the hardware its capability to function. Software gives the hardware a "personality," thereby creating a tool for information management. Software and hardware are inseparable. One cannot function without the other.

The many personalities imparted to a computer through its software are varied and fascinating. Thus, the selection of appropriate software to meet your pastoral ministry needs should not be taken lightly. While software selection is not complex, a methodical and analytical approach to the process lessens confusion, particularly for a pastor who is buying a computer for the first time.

Software Evaluation and Selection Factors

Selecting software is a subjective, qualitative process. There are many factors to consider when choosing appropriate software for your information needs.

The personal computer market has software packages that are generally satisfactory for pastoral ministry needs, but their evaluation will require substantial effort on your part. Some of these software packages are generic in nature so that they will work with several different hardware brands. Other software is machine specific, i.e., it will function only on one or two specified brands of hardware. Careful examination of available software based on the following factors is needed to help you find the right package for you.

Does it meet your needs?

The foremost factor to analyze in selecting pastoral software is to determine how closely the software meets your needs. Ideally, the software should exactly meet the needs identified in your pastoral information needs analysis. If such a software package can be found, it would fulfill your needs without any changes or adjustments. In reality, however, you probably will not be able to locate software that exactly meets your needs. Thus, you evaluate and choose the software that comes *closest* to meeting your ministry information management needs.

Is it user-friendly?

User-friendly software enables the computer operator (you) to use the software efficiently and effectively without referring constantly to the software manual or trying to solve a mystery that the software presents. User-friendly software never leaves you without an option, but always has a question or prompt that requires some response from you. Generally, if you try some software that seems cumbersome, it isn't user-friendly for your needs.

User-friendly software is typically "menu driven." A software menu is quite similar to a menu in a restaurant. It presents you with a number of choices and after examining the options, you are expected to make a choice. The choice you make may lead to another menu or move you immediately into some form of processing. Figure 4-1 displays an example of a menu.

Figure 4-1

Sample Menu

1. Membership Data Base
2. Personal Budget System
3. Sermon recording/retrieval
4. Return to main menu

Please enter selection:

Software user-friendliness is a matter of degrees. Some software is more user-friendly than others. Almost all software publishers claim their programs are user-friendly. However, user-friendliness is really a qualitative decision on the part of the user, and much software is obviously not user-friendly when you try it. Only by trying the software can you determine whether it is sufficient for your particular needs.

Integration

Integration or interfaced software refers to the degree in which programs work together to save processing time between applications. Integration in software applications reduces the amount of time and effort required in maintaining data. For example, if you need to enter a new name and address in the membership and pledge accounting systems, integrated software means it is not necessary to enter the name and address of the person twice for two different applications. Only one entry is necessary.

Like user-friendliness, integration is a matter of degrees. Some generic software, which includes many different functions, is able to achieve high levels of integration. Other software does not and should be carefully considered in light of the duplicated effort it may require in your information system.

Some highly integrated software packages use a concept called *multiple windows*. Multiple windows present several different applications on the computer at one time. If you change something in one window, it is automatically changed in the other windows at the same time, thus eliminating duplicated entries.

The multiple-window technique allows the user to have views of the same information in several different forms. For example, you can have two windows displayed on the computer's screen where the first window shows reference data on sermon illustrations. The other window displays the actual sermon you are currently writing and editing. The best part of the multiple-window technique in this example is that both windows appear on the computer's screen at the same time! This can be very helpful in organizing a sermon more effectively.

Documentation

Software documentation consists of manuals and other printed materials that explain how to use the software. You should examine these materials to make sure they are clear, precise, easy to read, easy to use, and understandable. They will be your computer reference guides much as *The Interpreter's Bible, Strong's Concordance,* or a Bible dictionary are reference guides for preparing sermons.

Reviews

Most popular generic software has been reviewed by competent professionals from various sources. Some reviews can be found in computer magazines, although reviews can also be purchased from computer services. The majority of reviews will rate the software and its quality in a variety of areas including user-friendliness, documentation, ease of use, and other features. Reviews can be helpful in your evaluation process and later in actually using the software.

References

If you are considering little known or customized software that has not been reviewed, then it would be wise to obtain references of others who are using the software. Talking with others who are using the software can provide useful information for your evaluation. If the vendor refuses to give you a reference list, then go to someone else. Refusal to provide references may indicate a problem-filled software package.

Demonstration

A "hands-on" demonstration of the software can provide you with a useful way of determining how well the software will meet your needs. (Hands-on means you actually work the software.) A hands-on demonstration will help you discover if the software is sufficient for your ministry information system. A hands-on demonstration can usually be done in a computer store; however, make sure the vendor allows you to do the actual work. A demonstration where the vendor does the work for you is not hands-on, but a sales pitch.

Support

Support primarily means that when you have a question or an error, someone is available to help you. Many software vendors offer toll-free telephone numbers that you can call to talk with someone about the difficulty you are experiencing. In other instances, no support of any kind is offered. Support depends upon the dealer and the original software publisher.

If you are already familiar with computers, support may not be an important issue. On the other hand, if you are new to the computer world, then support is vital to a successful pastoral computer operation. Consideration of this factor should be based upon your previous experience and level of comfort in dealing with computer problems when they arise.

Some questions to consider in the support area include:

— What is the procedure if something strange appears on the screen while using the computer?

— Is there a toll-free telephone number or support service that you can call if you are having a problem? How well does the toll-free support mechanism work?

— How much does support cost? Is the charge based on a per call, per hour, or per day rates? Is there a yearly maintenance fee for support, and what does that fee buy?

Training

Most computer vendors sell personal computers as appliance dealers sell televisions. When you get a new television, inside the box you will find an owner's manual that describes how the television works and what to do if something does not seem to be functioning properly. Most modern personal computers sold in today's neighborhood computer stores follow the same procedure. When you buy a computer, you will load several boxes into your car, take them home, unpack them and find numerous manuals that describe how to use the computer. It is up to you to read the manuals and make the computer operational.

Some vendors and computer stores offer a variety of training opportunities in the use of the computer or software you have purchased. These include:
— Classes at the vendor's location or office.
— On-site training at your church or in your home.
— Self-instructional materials included with the software.

Normally training costs additional money on a per hour, per day, or per class basis. You may find one or more of these training opportunities beneficial, depending upon how inclined you are to open manuals and find the answers you need to make your computer work. Training can be valuable in understanding how the software can provide optimum benefits for you.

Many software packages come with tutorials. A tutorial is an educational training technique that enables the user to learn how to use the software. The tutorial should be used if one comes with the software. Tutorials can help you see ways to use the software for ministry that might not be shown in other training opportunities.

Minimum Pastoral Software Requirements

The minimum software requirements for a pastoral computer system includes five basic units. Any of the pastoral computer applications described in this book can be accomplished with one of the five software packages described below. However, considerable work on your part may be required to make the applications described in chapters 9 to 12 function correctly.

The minimum software requirements for a pastoral computer system are:

1. Data base management
2. Report generator
3. Spreadsheet
4. Word processing
5. Security

Data base management

A data base is a collection of related information about a particular subject or general interest area. Software for a data base management system (DBMS) controls the data base so that particular information needs can be fulfilled. In other words, a DBMS enables you to store large amounts of information in a variety of ways to meet specified needs. Often a DBMS is considered relational, which means that it is possible to relate several different files of data in useful ways.

Report generator

A report generator enables the user to produce documents and reports in specified formats to meet particular needs. A report generator can manipulate title headings, columns, and rows of information so that your output is displayed on the screen or printed on the printer in formats that are useful for ministry. Report generators are often optional parts of a DBMS and make extensive use of sort routines.

Spreadsheet

Spreadsheet software allows the user to create large groupings of numerical data in rows and columns, and manipulate that data quickly and simply through mathematical techniques. A particularly helpful attribute of spreadsheet software is its ability to project budgets and future financial requirements based on current conditions. Specifically, spreadsheet software is useful for personal budgeting, filing of income taxes, and in projecting the church's budget.

Word Processing

Word processing software provides the user with an extremely sophisticated electronic typewriter that allows easy entry, editing, and printing of textual information without using a pen or pencil, requiring minimal amounts of paper. The proper use of word processing software almost eliminates the need for draft copies of a document that would have to be retyped in their entirety after editing. Thus, the total amount of paper needed in producing a document is substantially reduced.

A technique often used in word processing is called *document generation*. In document generation, name and address files can be transferred into word processing to produce personalized mass mailings. In other words, a letter can be sent to all church members that consists of the same text, but has individualized names, addresses, and salutations. Document generation will be discussed further in chapter 12.

Security

Security software protects your data from being seen (accessed) by unauthorized individuals. Security software is necessary because there is a possibility that a pastoral computer system will contain confidential information about church members (see chapter 13). Software designed for security purposes can be purchased separately, or it can be a part of the data base, report generator, spreadsheet, and/or word processing packages. It is best to ask your vendor about security protections included in the software you are considering for your pastoral information system.

Off-the-Shelf or Customized?

The software packages just described can be obtained either "off-the-shelf" from a computer dealer or can be customized for your needs. Off-the-shelf software means that you can purchase the software from a computer dealer when buying the computer. Customized software means that either you or someone else has written software to meet your specific pastoral ministry needs.

Note that it is always advisable to purchase an off-the-shelf word processing package, even if you choose customized software for the pastoral data base, report generator, and spreadsheet functions. Word processing software is difficult to customize and requires a computer professional to develop an efficient word processing package. Most off-the-shelf word processing packages are excellent for pastoral ministry information needs.

Off-the-Shelf Packaged Software

Many off-the-shelf software packages have useful features that can be quite helpful in a pastoral computer system with sufficient processing power to meet your needs. However, off-the-shelf software packages should be thoroughly examined using the factors previously discussed to determine just how useful they are for your ministry information needs.

When using this software, it is important to read the manuals and documentation carefully. Often a problem can be traced to the fact that the manual was misread or not read at all. Almost all of the questions that develop can be answered in the software's documentation IF the time is taken to find the answer. Even though the documentation may not be very user-friendly, the time invested in finding the correct answer will benefit the user with a deeper familiarity of the documentation. In addition, the user may discover some previously unknown feature of the software that could be extremely helpful in ministry information management.

Customized Software

As mentioned previously, customized software is specifically designed to meet the needs of the user. Customized software is a better choice than off-the-shelf software for a pastoral computer system because it is especially written for a pastor's information needs. Using a customized pastoral data-base/report generator system coupled with an off-the-shelf word processing package is probably the most powerful and effective software combination for a pastoral computer system.

There are four alternatives for obtaining customized pastoral ministry software:

1. The software can be purchased from a dealer or religious publishing house. Some church software dealers and vendors offer limited pastoral computer software that will accomplish a few of the applications suggested in this book.

   Advantages:

   —Probably less expensive than other alternatives.

  —Support will probably be better than other choices.

  —Will meet your needs better than generic software.

 Disadvantage:

  —May not meet your needs exactly.

2. You can design and write the software. In this option, you would learn a computer language that works on your computer, complete a systems analysis of your pastoral information needs, design the software according to your specifications, and actually do the programming.

 Advantages:

  —The software will meet your needs *exactly*.

  —New skills are gained.

 Disadvantages:

  —Very time-consuming, which reduces your availability for ministry.

  —New skills must be learned if you have no prior experience in systems analysis, design, and computer programming.

3. A free-lance programmer or software house can design and write the software on a contractual basis.

 Advantages:

  —The software will meet your needs *exactly*.

  —It will probably be comprehensive and well-written if the programmer is a professional and if the software house's business depends upon good products.

 Disadvantages:

  —Very costly, probably the most expensive alternative.

  —Support will probably be expensive.

  —Much time will be needed on the pastor's side to work with the programmer to provide him or her a detailed understanding of pastoral ministry information management.

4. A friend with programming skills could write the software.

Advantages:

—The software will meet your needs *exactly*.

Disadvantages:

—Time-consuming.

—A friend is being imposed upon for an extensive project.

—Confidentiality of information may be violated. This depends upon the trustworthiness of the friend.

—Support can be a problem due to:

   a. The excessive amount of time the friend may have to give to answer questions or correct problems.
   b. The possibility of the friend moving out of the community, making long-distance support impractical or even impossible.
   c. The friend's death.

The Software Headache

Attempting to choose software for pastoral ministry can be an intensely frustrating headache. However, it must be done. Thus, whether the final selection in your ministry is off-the-shelf, customized or a combination of both software types, a careful and thorough analysis is absolutely essential. The aspirin in reducing the headache is always to base all software decisions upon your pastoral ministry needs.

5

The Question of Hardware

*Do you not know that your body is a temple of the Holy Spirit
within you, which you have from God?*

I Corinthians 6:19

The final major step in acquiring a pastoral
computer system is the evaluation and selection of
computer hardware. Once you have chosen the
software, the choice of hardware becomes a relatively
simple and objective matter. If the software you have
chosen is machine specific, i.e., functions on only one
brand of hardware, then you purchase that hardware.
If the software works on more than one computer,
then you must evaluate and select hardware from
available options.

Hardware Evaluation and Selection Factors

The following section notes the numerous factors to
consider in hardware evaluation and selection. Hardware analysis should be grounded in the results of
your needs analysis using these factors.

Processor

The first generation of commercially available
micro-computers used 8-bit processors. These machines have almost disappeared from computer stores
but are readily available in the used market. The
second generation micro-computers consist of 16-bit
and 32-bit processors. It is generally more desirable to
obtain a computer with a 16- or 32-bit processor,

because additional features are available with the larger processors. In addition, the larger bit-size processors are faster and more efficient than 8-bit processors.

The used computer market should be seriously considered, and for most pastors, it may be the only way to afford a computer. However, when buying a used 8-bit computer, remember that the majority of existing software sold in computer stores will not function on these machines.

When considering the processor, your software will specify two items needed for operation: operating system and processor memory size. Both of these specifications must be met for your software to function.

Generally, 8-bit processors use the CP/M operating system. The 16- and 32-bit micro-computers use the CP/M-86, MS-DOS, and UNIX operating systems. CP/M and MS-DOS are de facto "standards," and most 8-bit software is CP/M based while most 16-bit software is MS-DOS based. The UNIX operating system is a very powerful operating system that will support subsets of MS-DOS and CP/M in many instances. With these subsets, applications designed under CP/M and MS-DOS will function under UNIX.

In addition to the operating system, a proper amount of processor memory is required to execute the software. For example, if the software requires 256K of processor memory, a 128K computer is not sufficient. You will need to add an additional 128K of processor memory to use the software. The amount of processor memory needed is a minimum, based on the software specifications. In other words, software needing 256K to execute cannot work in 128K, but can work in 512K.

Monitor

The computer monitor is the screen that the machine uses to communicate with you. Some micro-computers can use standard television sets as a monitor attached to the processor through an RF modulator device (RF means radio frequency). In other cases, a monitor manufactured by the vendor must be purchased as one component of the computer.

Monitors come in a variety of shapes, sizes, and colors—depending upon the needs and desires of the buyer. Some of these include the black and white, color, green, and amber background monitors. Non-color monitors are often called *monochromes*. If you have more than one monitor choice available, decide which is easiest for you to read over an extended period of sitting in front of the screen.

If you want graphics in your computer, then a monitor should be obtained that is capable of generating graphics in addition to your color choice. Graphics in a computer is the machine's ability to draw pictures and other visual representations of data such as bar and pie charts. Figure 5-1 contains examples of simple bar and pie charts.

To generate charts like those in Figure 5-1, graphics monitors must have high resolution. A high resolution monitor has the ability to fill in the spaces on the screen so that uninterrupted lines are shown.

Special function keys on the keyboard

Some computer keyboards have special function keys enabling the operator to use the machine more efficiently, particularly in word processing. For example, some keyboards have insert character, delete characters, insert line and delete line keys; these enable the machine to work more efficiently by

Figure 5-1

Examples of Pie and Bar Charts

PIE CHART

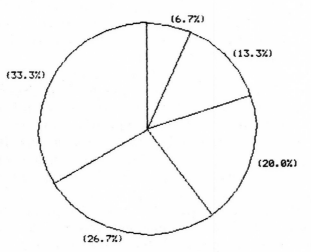

BAR CHART

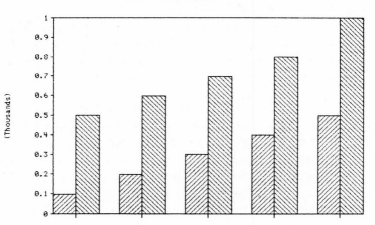

reducing the number of required operator keystrokes. In addition, most computer keyboards have "cursor" movement keys that allow you to move the cursor anywhere on the screen with ease. (The cursor is the small box or line on the screen where the characters appear when you press a key.)

You should determine what special function keys are available on the computer's keyboards you are evaluating and if those keys are useful for you. Substantial word processing applications generally call for special function keys to improve work efficiency.

Mass storage

Mass storage is a method of storing information so that it can be recalled at a later time. Mass storage is *required* in order to use a computer effectively. Many mass storage devices are available to store information in computers. These devices use magnetic fields on a special media to store data. (A media usually consists of a mylar-like product capable of recording magnetic impulses.) Mass storage devices store information using bit and byte codes. Using magnetic impulses and "ticks," data is placed on the media in a way that makes sense to the computer. Mass storage devices enable a computer user to store large amounts of information inexpensively in a small space.

You will need to select which type of mass storage device is the most beneficial for your needs because they come in three general types for micro-computers:

1. Cassette tape.
2. Floppy disk.
3. Hard disk.

You should probably avoid cassette tape as your primary storage device because tape is generally much slower and less efficient than using floppy or hard disks. However, cassette tape is also usually inexpensive in the beginning because a standard cassette tape recorder can be used with some micro-computers. For your long-term needs, though, it is better to purchase a computer with at least two floppy disk drives, or a hard disk and one floppy disk drive.

If you choose floppy disks, you will find that there are two popular sizes. The most prevalent standard floppy disk size is the 5¼-inch. A second and increasingly popular size of floppy disk is the 3½-inch. Other size floppy disks are available, but 5¼-inch and 3½-inch are the most commonly used in micro-computers.

The 3½-inch floppy disk has a different form than the 5¼-inch disk. The 3½-inch disk has a hard plastic shell casing to protect the media, unlike 5¼-inch disks, which use a soft plastic shell. Floppy disks of 5¼-inch and 3½-inch will typically store between 200,000 and 800,000 characters of information per disk.

The most expensive and most efficient storage media is a hard disk. Hard disks come in a variety of sizes depending upon the computer. The smallest hard disk generally available is 5 MB (1 MB = 1,000,000 characters). Larger size hard disks in micro-computers can hold 20 MB or more. Mainframe and mini-computers hard disks are capable of supporting hundreds of megabytes of storage on one disk, and some will even support gigabytes (GB), or billions of characters.

New developments in mass storage technology are constantly appearing in the micro-computer world. In the future, floppy and hard disks could easily be replaced at a fraction of the cost as new GB disk technology is perfected for micro-computers.

Printers

There are two primary qualities of print available with computers today:

1. Draft. Usually, draft printing uses the popular dot matrix format.
2. Letter quality.

Both dot matrix and letter quality printers are mechanical in nature. They are also impact printers—meaning that hammers press against a ribbon, which then hits against the paper to form a letter.

The dot matrix type printer produces a draft quality print that many people mistakenly call computer print. Draft quality print is used to produce working reports and drafts of word processing documents for editing purposes.

A letter quality printer is very much like a typewriter without a keyboard. Most good letter quality printers use a ball or wheel and generate print equal to or better than a regular office typewriter.

Some printers are also able to generate both draft and letter quality print. This type of printer can be very useful if you need both draft and letter quality output in your operation and want the convenience of both formats in one device.

The key to your printer decision is whether you need draft or letter quality print in your output. Typically a dot matrix printer is much faster and less expensive than a letter quality printer. However, if you are going to be sending letters produced by word processing, letter quality may be the better choice. It is a known fact that most people prefer letter quality over draft print. In many instances, when people receive a letter printed on a draft quality printer, they will respond by saying that they received a computer written letter.

When you select your printer, sensitivity to your congregation's preferences should be considered. This will help you decide which printer is best. If your computer is expandable, you can buy a draft quality printer in the beginning and a letter quality printer later as funds become available.

You should also be aware that some printers require special paper for printing. For example, thermal printers, which are draft quality, must have specially treated paper because a thermal printer burns the characters into the paper. You should check this because special paper is more expensive than regular paper.

Also, some printers will not **BOLD** or underscore. If you want to do printing with bolding or underscores, you must buy a printer capable of such features.

Some computer hobbyists advise first-time computer buyers to obtain a letter quality printer and use it for all printing. However, the professionals disagree with this because letter quality printers are not designed for long printing runs, such as labels and lengthy reports. Most letter quality printer manufacturers will tell you that their printers have a high probability of mechanical difficulties if used consistently for printing best done on draft quality printers. Thus, if you buy a letter quality printer rather than a draft quality printer in the beginning, be prepared to add a dot matrix or draft quality printer at a later time.

Like disk technology, new printer technologies are constantly appearing. These newer printers are more reliable because they use very few mechanical parts when compared to dot matrix and letter quality printers. In addition, the quality of print on the new printers is usually better than existing dot matrix or letter quality printers.

Another hybrid computer printer is the typewriter/printer. Some regular typewriters can also work as a letter quality printer from a computer. Typewriter/printers are versatile machines because they provide two functions in one. On the other hand, they have slow printing speeds and should not be used for large print runs, such as several hundred labels or document-generated letters.

The key in selecting a printer is to determine what best suits your pastoral ministry needs. Frustration will result if you fail to consider these needs.

Communications

Communications is where one computer "talks" with another computer, usually over a telephone line. Computer communications over a telephone line requires certain hardware and software. Communications between two computers in the same building can be done over a special cable, avoiding telephone lines altogether.

The primary hardware device necessary for computer communications over a telephone is a *modem*. A modem is a small electronic box that allows a computer to talk over a telephone line. A modem converts the data in your computer into an acceptable form for the telephone line. Modems are required at each end between the telephone line and the computer in order for the computers to communicate. You are responsible for the modem at your end while the computer owner at the other end is responsible for his or her modem. Figure 5-2 illustrates this concept.

Modems come in a variety of sizes, capabilities, and speeds. Some modems have intelligence in the form of micro-processors that enable you to program them for various functions. Other modems are simple devices that provide only one function—converting the data between your computer and the telephone line.

The most common transmission speeds on modems are 300 and 1200 bps. (Bps means the number of bits per second that are transmitted along the telephone line. A common synonym for bps is BAUD. Baud is a slang term for BPS; however, baud is used much more commonly than bps.) In order for the two computers to communicate, the modems must match transmission speeds.

Figures 5-2

**COMPUTERS USING MODEMS
TO COMMUNICATE**

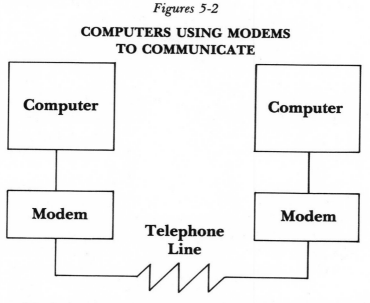

Modems may come as outboard devices that would be attached through cables to your computer and the telephone line. Modems may also be a circuit board that can be inserted into an available accessory slot in the computer. Your vendor can help you select the proper modem.

In addition to a modem, communications may also require software depending upon the computer. These software packages allow a computer to establish the necessary protocol information between computers. A communications protocol is a standard by which computers talk. Many protocols exist, and it is through the software that your computer establishes the necessary protocol controls so that communications can be achieved. Only your vendor will be able to tell if software is necessary for communications through your computer.

Interface

Hardware interfaces are standards by which different pieces of computer hardware can be connected by cables. For example, your computer needs an interface so that it may print information onto your printer. Your floppy disk drive needs an interface so that it may send information to and from the processor. Interfaces are often included within the computer so that you need not be overly concerned about this. However, some computers require certain interface cables and circuit boards in order to function. These you will have to add.

There are two primary types of interface used in micro-computers today: serial and parallel. The serial interface is primarily a cable that is generally designated by RS-232C. The parallel interface is usually designated by a cable that is called an IEEE-488. Parallel interfaces usually require a circuit board where serial interfaces usually do not. The need for additional circuit boards depends on the computer manufacturer. The vendor can tell you the exact circuit boards and cables needed to complete the hardware interfaces.

Generally, if you have an ABC computer but wish to use an XYZ printer with your computer (in a case where the XYZ printer is not made by the ABC computer company), then you will have to determine which interface is appropriate. Determining the proper interface is not difficult, but the interface itself will probably cost you additional money.

Maintenance

Computers occasionally break down, requiring maintenance. There are two primary types of hardware maintenance.

1. On-site service. In this type of service, a repair technician will come to your church or home and fix the computer if it breaks down. This type of maintenance requires a maintenance contract. Maintenance contracts are similar to an insurance policy. Payment of a monthly fee guarantees certain maintenance protection for your machine.

2. Depot maintenance. Depot maintenance is a carry-in type of service where the computer is physically taken to a service center for repair. Costs for depot maintenance are generally charged on a time and material basis.

Other types of maintenance are available, which basically combine a maintenance contract and depot maintenance. In a combined system, a monthly fee is paid for maintenance, but the machine is carried into a service center when it is broken. The maintenance contract in this situation guarantees certain protections such as twenty-four hour turnaround or that a "loaner" machine will be provided until yours is fixed.

Environment

The computer's environment consists of the physical specifications required to operate the hardware. You need to know these specifications so that if any special environmental requirements are necessary, your church or home can be adjusted accordingly. Most computer manufacturers specify environmental conditions in three areas:

1. Temperature. Manufacturers generally will indicate temperature in optimal, tolerable, and nonacceptable operating ranges for the computer. Frequently, the documentation will display a chart much like the one in Figure 5-3 to visually illustrate these temperature ranges.

Figure 5-3

Computer Temperature Specification Chart

45°	60°	80°	100°

```
<  ———      < ——— >  < ——— >  < ——— >     ——— >
```

Nonopera- tional	Tolerable	Optimal Operations	Tolerable	Nonopera- tional

2. Humidity. Most computers have operational humidity specifications. Charts with humidity specifications are similar to those that show temperature operating requirements.
3. Electrical. Some computers must meet certain electrical requirements to function properly. These requirements will indicate whether a normal electrical line in any household or office is sufficient for the computer or if the machine needs a totally dedicated electrical line. A dedicated electrical line is one which does not have *any* other electrical device attached (or plugged in) to it.

In addition to the temperature, humidity, and electrical requirements is the simple environmental problem of where in your house or office the computer will be placed, the size table needed for the hardware, and other physical considerations. More about physical environment is discussed in chapter 7. For all practical purposes, any micro-computer will operate in any church or home. However, to be safe and to avoid unexpected surprises later, knowledge about the computer's environmental restrictions will help you with your planning.

Expansion potential

It is likely that your information needs will change as you continue to use the computer in pastoral ministry. However, you may also find your computer incapable of supporting your growing and changing information needs. As a result, you may find it necessary to expand your computer. For example, a computer expansion may include the addition of a letter quality printer, another floppy disk drive, or perhaps a hard disk. Thus, you should examine the expansion potential of the computers you are considering.

Some computer manufacturers of professional level micro-computers allow several peripheral devices to be attached to their machines. Such capability permits combinations of two or three printers and several hard disk drives to be connected to the computer, depending upon your requirements. However, other less expensive popular home computers do *NOT* allow much expansion. Thus, only two floppy disk drives and one printer may be attached to the computer with no possibility of expansion beyond the initial purchase.

Reliability

Ask the vendor for references from those who have purchased the computers you are evaluating. You should then contact them to determine if the hardware has been reliable and functioned well. In addition, these references can also provide valuable information about the installation and start-up procedures, and thus help you watch for any unusual occurrences not explained in the manuals or by the vendor.

Documentation

As with software, it is important that the hardware documentation be clear and concise. The manuals will become your reference tools in explaining the hardware and how it is supposed to work. Carefully examining the documentation will help you determine if it is suitable.

Vendor stability

The financial stability of the dealer and manufacturer of the computer should be carefully considered. Many computer vendors and local dealers in the volatile micro-computer industry are here today and gone tomorrow. Vendor stability is important for future support.

Some questions to consider include:
—Is the local dealer reputable and financially stable?
—If you buy the computer from the only computer dealer in town and the dealer suddenly goes out of business, what support alternatives do you have?
—Is the original manufacturer well-known in the market?
—Does the manufacturer have a solid financial backing?

It is advisable when obtaining the hardware from a local dealer to buy a computer that has a major national support system behind it provided by the original manufacturer. This means that if the local dealer goes out of business, support can continue for your machine.

Reviews

As mentioned in the software chapter, many magazines also feature hardware reviews. Researching these reviews to determine how computer professionals rate the particular computer you are evaluating can prove invaluable. In addition, the reviews often provide extremely important information that the computer documentation does not. This information can be immensely helpful in trying to make your computer function properly in the pastoral ministry. Computer magazines can be purchased in computer stores and bookstores, and in some locales, even grocery stores sell computer magazines.

Minimum Pastoral Hardware Requirements

The *minimum* hardware requirements for a pastoral computer system includes six basic pieces:

1. The processor (CPU) with a minimum of 128K memory for generic, off-the-shelf software. If using generic or customized software requiring more memory, you will need to add enough processor memory to meet the specifications.
2. Two floppy disk drives.
3. A monitor. Perhaps a second or third television available in your home could function as a monitor. If you plan to use a television, then an RF modulator is required.

4. A keyboard, with special functions keys for word processing.
5. A printer. Print quality is based upon your needs, but a printer is absolutely essential for a pastoral computer system.
6. Cables for connecting (interfacing) the various hardware pieces together.

6

Dealing with Vendors

Behold, I send you out as sheep in the midst of wolves; so be wise as serpents and innocent as doves.

Matthew 10:16

Part of the computer selection process includes the inevitable visits to computer stores and conversations with computer sales representatives. While the factors described in the previous two chapters account for most of the issues in selecting a computer, the discussions held with a salesperson can sway you away from your original needs. The following advice is offered to help you deal with a computer sales representative as you make your final selection.

Computer Sources

Computers are available from a variety of sources which can be classified into two major groups—new and used computers. A new computer would be purchased from a computer store, while a used computer could be obtained from a store or private individual. The new computers are likely to incorporate state-of-the-art technology, depending on the manufacturer. Used computers utilize older technology, but may be perfectly adequate for your pastoral ministry needs. New computers will probably cost more money than used computers, depending upon the vendor or individual.

New computers can be obtained only from stores or dealers. As you can imagine, computer vendors come in many sizes, shapes, and sales pitches. Independent computer stores selling computers and related services are popping up all over the country. In addition, many kinds of retail and wholesale chain stores are offering computers to the public at large. Vendors should be treated in the same way, whether they are part of an independent computer store or a retail department store. They should know their product and, if they don't, go to another store.

Used computers can be purchased through computer hobbyist shows in your locale, by answering a newspaper advertisement, or through a friend familiar with the computer market. While many used computers may be adequate for the pastoral ministry, finding adequate software may be a problem. Some of the latest off-the-shelf or customized software will not work on a used computer. Thus, if you are interested in purchasing a used computer, be sure to examine the software very carefully, always basing the evaluation upon your needs.

Vendor Selection Factors

There are a number of factors about vendors to consider when contemplating the purchase of a computer. Choosing a vendor can be as important as selecting the right software and hardware.

Vendor knowledge

Some of the computer salespeople with whom you will deal have very little knowledge about the machines they sell. Many have only attended a one- or two-week sales seminar where they learned the features of the particular machine they are selling compared with others in the market. It may be hard to believe, but the sales seminar is the first time many sales people have ever seen a computer! You will quickly discover that some vendors know little about the specific machine they sell, about computers in general, and worst of all, about how a computer will benefit your ministry. After reading this book and talking with a salesperson, you may realize that you know more about the computer than the salesperson you talked to. You are probably right. The vendor often gives the impression that his or her interest is in selling you a computer for the lucrative commission rather than determining what software and hardware is best for your ministry needs. Ask some questions you know the answers to, and if the vendor can't answer them or gives wrong answers, go to someone else.

Software versus hardware

Though they may be well-meaning individuals, sales representatives are in the business of selling hardware. They have life-styles and families to support like everyone. However, most computer salespeople usually make a mistake in extolling the virtues of the computer hardware rather than adequately demonstrating the software features. For example, a vendor is likely to tell you that their XYZ Computer has a 256K processor while computer ABC sold by so-and-so has only 128K. In reality, the size of the processor memory really doesn't matter until you consider the software that will meet your ministry needs. If your software operates in 128K then it really does not matter that the XYZ computer has 256K. Thus, be wary when the sales representative tries hard to compare different hardware when your primary interest is in software.

Eventually, hardware comparisons are valid, but initially you need to ask software questions. If you keep asking questions about word processing features, data base functions, or spreadsheet capabilities, but the salesperson keeps returning to the hardware, then avoid that sales person and probably that store.

Once you have determined which software packages best suit your information needs as a pastor, then you can discuss hardware with the vendor. At this point, the salesperson should be able to tell you that the software you have selected will work on certain types of hardware. Then, compare the hardware and examine processor memory size, mass storage sizes and media, printing capacity, and other hardware features. Eventually, the machine that suits your needs best and gives the most for your money will present itself.

Negotiation

Most computer dealers significantly mark up the cost of a computer. In other words, there is usually room for negotiating the price. Clearly state to the sales representative why you want a computer and how you plan to use it. Then, when the time is appropriate, ask your vendor about the possibility of a discount on the system. Most vendors have discounts on the computer, depending upon the profit margins they have established.

In some instances, vendors may not give hardware discounts, but may include certain software packages at "no cost" with the entire system. Software at no cost should be considered in light of its relative value and usefulness to you. For example, a good word processing package included at no cost could be a five-hundred-dollar value.

You should also consider paying a little more to a store with a professional and helpful staff. The investment in a computer from that store is certainly worth more than a super discount offered by a store that treats its customers like cattle in a slaughterhouse. The extra 10 percent spent initially will pay for itself in the future when the store's staff is easy to work with and courteous.

Check it out

Even if you think the vendor has offered a good deal on the computer, don't necessarily believe it is. Some salespeople can make a bad deal sound good. Therefore, once you have identified the particular software and hardware you wish to purchase, ask a friend you can trust or a computer professional you may be acquainted with to review the quote and make suggestions. An opinion from a third party will help you clarify whether the deal is as good as it sounds. You can also do some comparison shopping at several computer stores to verify the price.

Package deals

Be wary of some package deals offered by the vendor. A package deal usually includes hardware, software, and some starting supplies. Take a careful second and third look at any package deal to see if it truly represents the savings the vendor claims.

Certain package deals can be the vendor's attempt to reduce inventory because he or she is aware of impending price decreases or soon to be released new products reducing the value of the system being sold to you. A really good package deal could be a ploy when, two weeks later, the price for everything you are buying will be five hundred dollars less than the package deal is in the first place!

Also, be very careful to examine the software that may be included in a package deal. Vendors have been known to slip old software releases in package deals to reduce inventory rather than including the latest version of the software available, even though he or she originally demonstrated the latest version to you. This means you could get a software system that is not functioning properly or does not have the features you expected. For example, it is possible the vendor demonstrated Word Processing Release 2.2, but sells you Release 2.0, which doesn't do everything 2.2 does. As a result, you end up with a less adequate software package because the vendor sold you a previous release. This can be a very frustrating surprise.

Some package deals also include more software than you can possibly use. The package may include three different spreadsheet programs, two different word processing programs, and four different data base systems. It is improbable you will use all these programs, but their cost is included in the package price. Why pay for something you will never use?

Use your needs analysis

Take your needs analysis results with you when you go to the computer store. The needs analysis will help you and the salesperson pinpoint how the computer will be used in pastoral ministry. The needs analysis results should help the vendor review and recommend available software to best meet your needs. It will help you focus on the features you really need and avoid the features you don't need. If the sales pitch sounds memorized, then the salesperson is not paying attention to your needs analysis. Having the needs analysis results in front of you will help to keep the vendor's sales pitch in perspective with your original plans.

Vendor defined needs?

As the pastor, you are responsible for knowing what you want in a computer. Your needs analysis will define the data required for your ministry information management system. Thus, it is extremely important that the vendor does not define your needs. For example, a preprogrammed demonstration may be "neat," but you need to work the computer yourself not using demonstration software. A vendor that defines your needs can lead you to the purchase of an inadequate computer system.

Warranties

What warranty and legal guarantees are offered with the computer systems you are examining? Usually personal computer manufacturers offer limited warranties from thirty to one hundred and twenty days. Also, some manufacturers offer the opportunity to purchase an extended warranty on the computer. However, extended warranties are similar to a service contract. Make sure the warranties and service claims are in writing. The responsibility is yours as the buyer to know what the warranties that come with the machine offer. Be sure you read and understand the fine print!

Material and supplies

A constant amount of supplies is needed for an effective computer operation. Generally, supplies include consumable items such as paper, floppy disks, printer ribbons, letter quality wheels, etc. Does the computer store or dealer who sold you the computer stock all of the needed supplies and materials? How much do they cost? Are ample supplies maintained in stock, or do they have to be ordered?

You may discover several pastors, churches, or church members using computers in your area who also need computer supplies. It may be beneficial to form a purchasing cooperative with others using computers to gain greater discounts through quantity purchases. For example, computer paper and printer ribbons can be often obtained at a 60 percent discount off the retail price when twenty boxes of paper are purchased. If ten people or organizations in a cooperative each need two boxes of paper, everyone realizes the cost savings. Thus, a cooperative could be extremely helpful in reducing the long-term cost of supplies.

Are you uneasy with the vendor?

If you become uncomfortable or uneasy with the sales representative or begin to have misgivings that he or she does not have your best interests at heart by pressuring you to buy before you are ready, then don't buy a computer from that person or store. Other alternatives are available. You make the ultimate decision. You have the final responsibility for your computer. You are entering into a long-term relationship with a particular computer store and if you are not comfortable, then look elsewhere.

7

Checkbook Realities

Jesus said to them, "Render to Caesar the things that are Caesar's, and to God the things that are God's."

Mark 12:17

The dollar cost for computers can overwhelm first-time computer buyers, particularly since they often assume that the advertised cost of a computer is the only expense involved. Most people think that a computer purchase is much like buying a microwave oven. You go to the store, pay five hundred dollars, bring the oven home, plug it in, and use it. Even though options are available for microwave ovens, such as special utensils and dishes, the options are not necessary. You have paid the five hundred dollars, have a fully operational microwave oven, and have no additional costs except for the minimal amounts of electricity needed to run the machine. Most consumers believe that when you purchase a product, it will work without additional cost. In other words, a check is written for a certain amount of money, and a product is received. Thus, first-time computer buyers always naively ask, "How much does it cost?"

All Is Not as It Appears

Advertised computer prices can be deceiving. The advertising copy says that you or your church can purchase a particular computer for X number of dollars. On the other hand, after going to the computer store, you discover that the advertised amount includes only the keyboard and processor!

Despite the vendor's claim, the computer does not function. It does not include every piece of hardware or software needed to make the machine a functional tool. Thus, this sort of advertising can often anger and frustrate computer buyers because they feel they have been deceived.

As a pastor, buying a personal computer for the first time can be a perilous journey in terms of cost. Don't limit yourself to the question "What does it cost?" It is incorrect to assume there are no more expenditures after the check is written. Rather, the question should be "What is the cost of the minimum amount of hardware, software, supplies, and environment controls necessary to meet my initial needs?" After these minimums have been determined, then you can calculate the total initial investment.

Computer Cost Categories

In the computer world there are two major categories of dollar cost: initial and long-term. Both of these cost areas should be considered when you plan your personal or church computer budget.

Initial costs

The initial costs of a computer system include all software, hardware, supplies, and environmental components obtained when the machine is first purchased. Two reasons make it difficult to estimate the exact bottom line for the initial cost of your computer system:

1. The components of your system depend entirely upon your needs. Your computer system should be configured to meet the pastoral ministry information management needs you have de-

fined. Some pastors will have a longer list of requirements than others, thus generating greater initial costs.

2. The computer market changes so rapidly that a computer selling for two thousand dollars now may cost only five hundred dollars in twelve months.

While I cannot provide you with an exact initial cost for your system, the following factors will help you determine the bottom-line initial cost of your system. Consider each of these factors in light of your needs.

Software

The cost of computer software will vary depending upon your needs. As discussed in chapter 4, the software needed to complete the pastoral applications listed in this book include:

1. Spreadsheet applications—$25 to $1,000.
2. Date-base management—$25 to $2,500.
3. Report generator—$25 to $500 if not included with the data-base software.
4. Word processing—$100 to $2,000. The word processing software should include a document generator. If the word processing package doesn't have a document generator, then you will need to spend an additional $100 to $500 for this option.
5. Security—$50 to $250, if not included in the above packages.
6. Customized pastoral software—variable depending upon needs.

The software listed above should be sufficient for pastoral purposes; however, you may also discover that additional software is needed to achieve the effectiveness you desire. The cost of each of these software packages will have to be included in your initial cost calculations.

Hardware

As discussed in chapter 5, the following hardware is the minimum needed for your work:

1. The processor (CPU) with the minimum memory required to meet the specifications.
2. Two floppy disk drives.
3. A monitor. If you plan to use a television in your home, an RF modulator will have to be purchased instead of a full monitor.
4. A keyboard.
5. A printer, either draft or letter quality.
6. Cables.

Other hardware may be required depending upon your needs. For example, in the area of communications over a telephone line, a modem will be needed, as well as some additional communications software.

Environmental Costs

Your initial cost outlay may also include some environmental costs—such as the installation of adequate temperature mechanisms, a dehumidifier or air conditioner to keep humidity in your computer room within certain levels, and the installation of adequate electrical lines. See chapter 5 for a more detailed discussion of the temperature, humidity, and electrical requirements of computers.

Another environmental factor relates to computer furniture. Obviously, a table or desk with chair is needed for the computer. You may wish to purchase a desk specifically for your computer. Many retail furniture stores sell computer desks.

You could also be creative when it comes to computer furniture and pirate an old, unused kitchen table in your home for the computer. (That's what I did!) Using existing furniture in your home probably means you need to improvise in several ways. For example, a small platform on the larger table may be needed to hold computer accessories and the printer so additional space can be found on the table. Such a platform can be built out of wood scraps, or perhaps a small fold-up table will work. Filing cabinets are also useful for keeping manuals and output. However, whether buying a new desk or improvising with an old kitchen table, some initial computer furniture expenditures will probably be necessary.

Supplies and Materials

Initial supplies including paper and floppy disks are necessary. Sometimes, the vendor will include a starter kit of supplies and materials with the purchase of a computer. However, in most cases you will need to buy paper, disks, and other items necessary to begin a computer operation.

Telephone

If you plan to use the computer in communications, then a telephone line is needed. The existing telephone in your home or study is sufficient if:

—Your calls to other computers are short so people trying to call you won't always encounter a busy signal.

—The line doesn't have an extension on it. An extension picked up by someone else while you are using the line with the computer can cause unpredictable and disasterous results.

If these two conditions cannot be met, then a separate telephone line is needed for the computer. Include this initial cost in your planning even though the cost for a telephone line installation is relatively small.

Initial Bottom-Line Cost

After you have determined the cost in each of the areas just discussed, the total is determined by adding the area costs together. Figure 7-1 shows an example of initial costs in a computer purchase.

Figure 7-1

Initial Bottom-line Cost Calculation

Software	$1,595
Hardware	2,495
Environment (including furniture)	350
Supplies and materials	85
Telephone	25

Total Initial Cost	$4,550

Please note that the example in Figure 7-1 is only an example. Your initial cost for a pastoral computer could be much less or greater depending upon your needs.

Long-term costs

The second cost category in a pastoral computer operation consists of the long-term expenditures. Organizations that have used computers for many years realize that computer technology costs money. However, most first-time personal computer owners discover this checkbook reality quickly and often rudely.

As an analogy, when an automobile is purchased, a major initial expenditure is required. However, to operate the car the gasoline tank must be filled periodically, the oil changed regularly, the engine tuned up annually, broken parts must be fixed, a license purchased, and an insurance premium paid. All of these items cost additional money that must come out of your resources.

Like automobiles, a computer requires a long-term dollar commitment in addition to the initial expenditure. The long-term costs for personal computers in the pastoral ministry are found in the following areas.

Software

Long-term software costs include:

—New releases of software originally purchased with the machine. The original publishers of most software periodically produce new software releases. New software releases are sometimes automatically sent to you at no cost. In other instances, the new release is provided upon the payment of a $50, $100, or $200 upgrade fee.

—New software purchases. As you become more skilled using the computer in ministry, new software packages can help meet a specific need that you previously have not been able to meet. The price of new software will vary depending upon the application and purpose.

—Customized software. If you develop your own software, your time is an indirect cost, which would be difficult to calculate. On the other hand, you will pay a fee for this service if you have software that is programmed specifically for your needs by a friend or a local programmer.

—Software support mechanisms. Many software support services charge a monthly fee. Some software support services charge between $5 to

$30 per month for unlimited support. Others charge on a per call, per hour, or per day basis.

Materials

Another long-term computer cost consists of supplies and materials. As mentioned previously, materials include floppy disks, printer ribbons, computer paper, etc.

Resources

After installing the computer, you will probably discover magazines, journals, books, and other printed materials about computers that are extremely valuable. In addition, you may wish to join a users' group with common interests in pastoral computing. Long-term costs for subscriptions or dues should be anticipated as additional resources about your pastoral computer system are discovered.

Maintenance

The types of computer maintenance are discussed in chapter 5. Maintenance of computer hardware does, however, add to the long-term cost of a computer operation. In general, hardware maintenance costs are:

—Maintenance contract: 0.5-2 percent per month of the original hardware cost. For example, if your hardware originally cost $5,000, then a maintenance contract will be between $25 and $100 per month.

—Depot maintenance is based upon time and materials usually with a minimum time charge of one hour. Hourly rates are generally between $40 and $150 depending upon the repair center and your geographic location.

—A combination maintenance contract with depot maintenance is less expensive than a regular maintenance contract, costing between 0.1 percent and 1.0 percent of the original hardware cost.

Communications

Commercially available data-base services or electronic bulletin board services to share information with other computer users require long-term expenditures. These costs include:

—The telephone call to the service. You pay the toll charge if it is a toll call at the same rates as a voice toll call. Note that many of the alternative long-distance services that are cheaper than traditional telephone companies (primarily AT&T) have notoriously poor reliability for computer communications. Thus, it may be best to avoid using the alternative telephone long-distance services for your computer communications until their reliability and data integrity improve.

—The cost of connect time to the service's computer. Connect time is usually computed on a per hour basis. Some hobbyist bulletin boards, however, are free.

—The initial and/or annual membership fee. The membership fee is usually between $25 and $200 depending upon the service.

—The regular monthly rental fee for any separate telephone line installed for the computer.

Who Pays for It?

At some point, you will have to decide if purchasing a pastoral computer system will come out of your own personal funds or if you want the church to buy the machine. This decision should not be taken lightly, particularly in a smaller church where funds may be less abundant. Someone or some group has to pay for it.

If you buy the computer out of your personal funds, there are several advantages and disadvantages.

Advantages:

—You own the computer. When you move, it moves with you.

—You have complete control. You make all decisions about the computer.

—Some tax breaks may be available. (See the next section.)

Disadvantages:

—When you move, the pastor who follows you is at a disadvantage if he or she doesn't have a computer. Even if your successor has a computer, chances are slim that it will be compatible with your computer, making data transfer almost impossible.

—Certain church members may pressure you to use the computer for church work other than in the pastoral ministry such as printing labels or keeping the church's financial records. If you refuse, problems may result.

—You have to pay all costs.

Advantages and disadvantages of the church owning the pastoral computer are:

Advantages:

—The church pays all costs.

—It is available to your successor with all data intact.

Disadvantages:

—You can't take it with you when you move. Thus, you may have to convince your new congregation to buy a pastoral computer.

—The church has control and can decide to use the computer for purposes other than pastoral. This could hinder your ministry, particularly if you have become dependent upon the computer.

Tax Breaks

If you personally purchase the computer, some and possibly all of your computer costs can be deducted from your income taxes when used for business purposes in the United States. Your computer expenses may qualify for an investment credit and depreciation depending upon your situation. Consultation with a tax accountant or lawyer will help you determine if you qualify for a deduction or tax credit. If you are a citizen of a country other than the United States, checking on your country's tax laws may yield unexpected financial benefits from your computer expenses.

The Costs Go On . . .

As I'm sure you are beginning to grasp, a personal computer for pastoral ministry can be an expensive venture. Be prepared to spend a significant amount of personal and/or church funds for this expensive tool. Every pastor who decides to use a computer will have different costs. Some costs will be greater and others less, but every pastor will have some long-term costs associated with his or her computer.

SECTION 3

COMPUTER APPLICATIONS
IN THE PASTORAL
MINISTRY

8

On Your Mark, Get Set and . . . GO!

Let us run with perseverance the race that is set before us.
Hebrews 12:1

The possible applications of a computer in pastoral ministry are limited only by the pastors's imagination and creativity. In general, any information a pastor keeps that can be organized into an orderly format can be processed by a computer. Such information can range from objective name and address data of individual church members to subjective two- or three-sentence descriptions of sermons. Potential computer applications should provide ways in which information is processed in an organized manner to significantly benefit ministry.

The following four chapters contain many possible applications of the computer to the pastoral ministry. The suggestions that follow are based on my overall view of ministry as a pastoral generalist with specialist skills in computer sciences and on my specific experience as a local church pastor. In other words, the suggested applications are intended as idea generators to get you started with a computer. As you consider these ideas in relationship to your own ministry, remember that the computer is a tool that enables a pastor to become more effective in his or her ministry.

Computer Applications in Pastoral Ministry

The applications of a computer to the pastoral ministry can be divided into four primary categories based upon a pastor's work. These are:

1. Pastoral—those tasks which place a pastor in the role of being a shepherd. These would include counseling, ministry in crisis situations—including deaths and accidents, visitation, etc. These tasks are generally accomplished in one-to-one situations between a pastor and another person, or in group settings such as a church school class or a family in a crisis situation.

2. Worship—primarily related to the Sunday morning worship experience that every pastor usually leads. In that worship experience, the pastor generally is the preacher but could also serve as the liturgist and fill other worship leadership roles.

3. Sermon—those tasks primarily related to the development, storage, and retrieval of sermons.

4. Administrative—those administrative and organizational tasks a pastor needs for daily ministry. Most churches either explicitly or implicitly define the pastor as the chief administrative officer of the church. This means the pastor is expected to provide general oversight for all recordkeeping, facilities management, financial concerns, and trouble-shooting. Such work usually requires large amounts of paper work. Some tasks included in this area would be answering letters, completing judicatory reports, ordering church school materials, maintaining the official record of church members, ordering supplies for the church office, and other administrivia.

These four work areas naturally overlap and interface at many points. The common bond in them is the motivation of the pastor to serve the church. This results in a dynamically interrelated management information system focused on one task—being a pastor.

Other ministry work areas may exist, but will probably be found in each individual pastor's style. In other words, not all pastoral work is necessarily broken into the four general areas of pastoral, worship, sermons, and administrative. The four work areas are not meant to be comprehensive, but to provide a starting point for you to begin an automated pastoral ministry information system.

Applications Conventions

The following chapters are broken into the four general areas just listed:

Chapter 9 — Pastoral
Chapter 10 — Worship
Chapter 11 — Sermons
Chapter 12 — Administrative

Each suggested application is discussed in relationship to several groupings or conventions.

1. General comments. A general description of the suggested application.
2. Suggested data items to be maintained. A listing of data items that relate to the application. The data items listed are usually meant as minimums for the application unless otherwise stated. Each pastor can add to the list depending upon his or her needs.
3. Possible reports and other output documents. This section suggests ways for using the application and for producing needed reports.
4. System comments. A brief description of how the suggested applications may fit into an overall ministry information system design for computer planning purposes.

5. Primary software. The key software package that will provide the necessary computer power to complete the suggested application.
6. Secondary software. Additional software that may enhance the application, but is not required for its completion.

9

Pastoral Computer Applications

*But whoever would be great among you must be your servant,
and whoever would be first among you must be slave of all.
For the Son of man also came not to be served but to serve.*
                                            Mark 10:43b-45

The potential of a computer in your ministry is only limited by your style of ministry. The pastoral tasks of ministry relate directly to the pastor/parish relationships you have with the congregation. The relationships, created through pastoral tasks, are vital for ministering to the church members. These relationships include the familiarity a pastor develops with individual parishioners, as well as the mastery he or she has with grasping the corporate thoughts and expressions of the congregation as a community of faith. In other words, effective ministry is only possible when a pastor understands his or her parishioners. To say it more succinctly, pastoral duties lead a pastor to be a shepherd that cares and nurtures the flock.

Many different kinds of information are required to pastor a congregation. All of the information is data about the people you serve. The variety of data you need to be an effective pastor is personal and confidential in many instances (see chapter 13) and is public in others. In addition, the accuracy of the data must be guaranteed if the integrity of your ministry is to be assured. The information must also be carefully organized to create optimal time for ministering, while the time required for information management including data analysis is kept to a minimum.

Several possible pastoral computer applications are presented in the following pages to help you understand how a computer can be specifically used. These include:

—Membership Data Base
—Ministry to the Bereaved
—Ministry in Crisis Situations
—Birthday and Anniversary Recognition
—Calling
—Counseling
—Premarital Counseling
—Evangelism
—Membership and Confirmation Training
—Sunday Worship Attendance Records.

Your style of ministry will define exactly how the computer is used in your personal pastoring techniques. Hopefully, the pastoral computer applications suggested in this chapter will not limit you, but touch a spark that lights the creative fires of your imagination.

Membership Data Base

General comments

The cornerstone of any pastoral computer system is accurate information about church members. Membership information is frequently disorganized and discovered by the pastor in random, unexpected ways. Once the information is learned, it is often maintained in a mental notebook, which can increase the risk of confusing one family with another and probably reduces the accuracy of the information. Yet, membership information is absolutely essential. Without church member data, a pastor cannot function.

The manual or mental maintenance of church membership information can be costly and time-consuming, depending upon your needs and memory capacity. Using a computer as an extension of your memory reduces the amount of time needed to organize membership information and increases the accuracy, reliability, and efficiency of the data. These benefits then should produce increased effectiveness in your ministry.

The individual pieces of information maintained in a computer membership data base consist of many aspects in a church member's life. However, the temptation to keep TOO much data on each member will be large. Information overload can develop if too much data is stored on each church member. Having too much data at your fingertips can make processing the data difficult and reduce the ways of making the information meaningful for your ministry. Too much information is confusing, and instead of saving you administrative effort, additional work is created! This defeats the purpose of using a computer in ministry, because the maintenance of membership information consumes more time rather than less when compared with a manual system.

Too much versus too little information is a dilemma. The key is to decide what is the minimum amount of membership information needed for a successful and meaningful ministry. Thus, to design a membership data base, first make a list of each item to be maintained. Include only that information that is useful to your ministry at the present time. Additional data can always be added at a later time if needed.

For example, most existing church information systems contain a data item or field for a church member's birthday. The birthdays of church members are important so that they can be recognized when their special day arrives. However, some church information systems also maintain the birthplace of church members in addition to the birthdays. Does maintaining the birthplace of each church member create opportunities for better pastoral ministry? If the answer is no, why waste time by including the birthplace of church members in the computer? Maintenance of any useless data takes valuable time and consumes extra disk space.

The issue here is not whether the birthplace of church members is important. It is important to the church member. The issue is whether birthplace is important enough for your pastoral ministry to include it in your membership data base. In other words, your membership data base should include only those data items that will help you to be a more effective pastor. The MINIMAX principal should apply to your beginning data base design. The minimum number of data items is also the maximum. Too little or too much information can detract from the original purpose of a computer—to improve pastoral ministry.

Suggested data to be maintained

The suggested data fields below are samples of what might be maintained in a membership data base. Your own ministry needs should be the ultimate guide you use. (NOTE: A *field* refers to each data item—a *record* of information contains all data on one person and a *file* contains all data of all church members.)

Family surname
Given names of individual this record pertains to
Address
Telephone number
Resident or nonresident status, e.g., a church
    member who is a college student or in the military
    would be nonresident
Infant (pre-school), child, youth, adult, or senior
Age

Birthdate

Marital status if adult

Anniversary date, if married

Education

Occupation and employer, work address and telephone number

Date of baptism

Date of church membership

Membership status, e.g., full, probationary, communicant, etc.

How gained membership, e.g., profession of faith, transfer, confirmation

Pledge and giving status

Current church committee memberships, current leadership positions

History of past church committee memberships and leadership positions

Record of church attendance during the current year

Date of last pastoral call

Calling zone

Special interests, skills, and hobbies

Participation in community activities outside of the church, both past and present

Brief medical history, e.g. personal physician, hospitalizations, allergies

Preferred salutation in document-generated mass mailings

Possible reports and other output documents

Reports from the membership data base will vary and are directly based upon your needs. You should choose reports that will help with particular projects. On the other hand, it is very easy to have computer output grow into mounds and mounds of information and paper. Some of the information may be useful and some may not. Thus, your reports should be generated on a need-to-know basis. Common sense should be used when producing reports from the membership data base so that information overload does not occur.

Any report discussed with any application can appear either on the computer's screen or printer. Use the screen if only one piece of information is needed about a certain church member. However, if you want a list of all information in the data base for updating purposes, then the printer would be used. Whether a report goes to the screen or to the printer will depend upon your individual needs and likes or dislikes.

Here are two examples of possible reports from the membership data base:

1. Suppose you are planning for the election of several new members to the church's finance committee. A woman with financial background is a member of the church who you believe is a good candidate for the committee. However, you have only been the pastor at the church for one year and wonder if she has served on the finance committee prior to your coming to the church. So you go to the computer and ask it to display the woman's membership information on the screen. From this screen report, you discover that she served twelve years on the finance committee and finished her term just before you became pastor. Thus, you decide to ask another person who has not yet served on the committee, but has expressed interest in the committee. You have saved time and the information in the membership data base has enabled you to make a more informed decision. (NOTE: When you ask the computer to provide some information, it is frequently called a "query" or "inquiry.")

2. Suppose someone in the congregation visits you one day in your study and suggests that it would be great to form a singles group of persons between twenty and thirty-five years of age. You agree that this is an excellent idea and ask what you can do to help the group get started. Your church member responds by asking who are the singles in the church between twenty and thirty-five. You say to wait just one minute while you turn to the computer. You then command the computer to generate a report on the printer that alphabetically lists all single persons in the congregation between these ages. You also ask the computer to include the addresses, telephone numbers, and some other miscellaneous data about each person in the report. The computer clicks and whirs for a few seconds (or minutes) and then begins to print. After the printer has stopped, you tear off a two-page report that lists eighty-two persons in the category you requested. Your church member is amazed at the speed in which you were able to produce the needed information and even more amazed that there are eighty-two potential candidates for this group. He becomes even more enthusiastic and wonders if you and he could compose a letter to be sent to the eighty-two persons inviting them to the first meeting. You say yes and turn to the computer once again. Through word processing, you compose a letter introducing the group as a new fellowship opportunity designed for singles. After the letter is completed, you ask the computer to once again generate the eighty-two names, but this time put the name and address information directly into the letter. Presto! You produce eighty-two personalized letters inviting

the reader to a new form of ministry in the church. Your church member is absolutely flabbergasted and becomes a strong defender of using new technology in the church. (NOTE: This process could be simplified by creating a disk file of all the names and addresses when the report was generated the first time. Then the disk file can be merged with the letter without needing to generate the names and addresses a second time.)

A church directory can also be produced from your membership data base. This directory, however, would be one that would serve your specific needs as pastor and is not necessarily a directory that would be distributed to the congregation. A congregational directory should be produced from the church's computer system if one exists. However, if your church doesn't have a computer, a church-wide directory can also be created from your pastoral membership data base if needed.

Regardless of the type of reports needed, you may wish to design exactly how those reports will look. For example, do you wish to list reports alphabetically by name? Or do you want to list a report alphabetically by name within age groups? Report generation software is usually required to produce reports in different ways from the same data base.

System comments

As you assemble your membership data base, remember that this base is the foundation of most pastoral and administrative applications discussed in this book. Therefore, it is important that significant thought, careful analysis, and reflective time be given to the development of the membership data base. If the original design is faulty and does not meet your pastoral needs, then it is probable that your pastoral ministry will become less effective because the computer system is consuming more time than it should.

If the church already has a computer, then most if not all of the data needed for your membership data base may already be available through the church's system. The church's membership data could be transferred to your computer, if the compatibility problems can be solved (see chapter 13). Using data that already exists will save considerable time with the initial entry of membership data. In addition, as the membership data is updated on the church's computer, you can "down-load" the new data and automatically update your membership data-base files on the pastoral computer. This process will save considerable maintenance of the data base files.

To accomplish the transfer of data between your computer and church's computer, you may need to develop customized software. However, the expense and time needed to develop customized software for transferring the data could be more costly and time-consuming than directly entering the data. In this case, you should go ahead and enter the data directly into your computer and maintain it as changes occur.

Another method to transfer data between computers is to share it through a networking technique. A network between micro-computers enables one computer to use data files contained in another computer. Networking is usually transparent to the user. In other words, you would not know it is happening.

In a network, the operator requests the data needed from the computer and if the machine does not find the data on its currently loaded disks, then it searches the disks of the other computers in the network until it finds the data that has been requested. This concept is popularly referred to as a Local Area Network or LAN. The "local" part means that the computers must usually be within one thousand feet of one another for the LAN to function.

Primary Software (Required):

Data base management

Report generator

Word processing, if using the data base in mailings

Secondary Software (Optional):

Local area network, if data is to be shared with the church's computer

Customized

Ministry to the Bereaved

General Comments

Perhaps one of the most crucial areas where a pastor can be of significant help is when there is a death in the congregation. The pastor can bring a word of hope and faith to grieving family and friends—a word that witnesses the powerful love of Christ.

When a death occurs, the need of the mourners is immediate. The pastor must be prepared to provide the necessary word of grace at a moment's notice. The pastor also has immediate needs. Accurate data must be secured quickly so that an appropriate response can be made.

The computer can provide you with data about the deceased and the family. This information could include notes about counseling sessions, membership data (including present and past service to the church), and other data that you define. Armed with such data, a more informed pastoral response can be made that helps you remain rational and level-headed in such an emotionally charged situation.

After the initial response to the immediate crisis, the computer can help with the detailed funeral preparations. The computer can also be used after the funeral to record observations and reactions about the family to determine if the grieving process is concluding naturally and whether additional pastoral counseling may be needed.

Suggested data to be maintained

Name of deceased member
Address
Marital status
Spouse's name, if married or divorced
Children's names and ages, if any
Grandchildren's names and ages, if any
Church membership data, including data of baptism, date of church membership, category of membership, committees served on, leadership positions held, special donations made, etc.
Date of last pastoral call, notes from last call
Hospital patient record
Favorite scripture and hymns
Additional comments

Possible reports and other output documents

Several reports and other documents can be produced that would be beneficial in the event of a death. For example, a report that contains the information shown in the previous section could be helpful in talking with the family. However, selecting only the data items you feel would be useful in your particular situation should also be possible.

Using word processing, several documents can be generated for the funeral, memorial, and/or burial service. These documents could include:

—A funeral sermon or meditation.

—An order of worship for the funeral service.

—A list of selected poems, illustrations, and other items relevant to the service.

Another document that can be helpful is a follow-up report. Follow-up reports are generally used at a later time. A follow-up report when someone dies is stored in a tickler file. (A tickler file contains notes and dates used to remind you of something in the future.) As an example, a tickler file or report in a bereavement case could remind you of the anniversary of the church member's death. After the funeral and the friends have left, the family and spouse of the deceased are still grieving. The grief can be especially stressful on the first anniversary of the death. A pastoral response at this time can provide much comfort and help when it seems everyone else has forgotten, and no one is there to support the spouse or children. The anniversary date of a death can be maintained manually on the pastor's calendar, but this can be a time-consuming and tedious task. If the date is kept in the computer, a tickler report can be generated each month that contains certain data useful in making a follow-up pastoral call one year later. The information in this report might include:

Name of deceased

Date of death

Date of funeral, memorial, and/or burial services

Location of internment

Spouse's name, address, and telephone number

Children's name, address, and telephone number

Age at death

Cause of death

Memorials received and resultant actions by the church memorial committee

Action taken by you as the pastor. This can be a checklist that you would later enter into the computer. It might include a telephone call, letter, card, visitation, and/or any other valid pastoral response.

System comments

This application can and should be integrated with other computer applications. These might include the church's membership data base maintained on the church's or on the pastor's computer, word processing for easy insertion of poems and illustrations into sermon text, and finances—particularly memorial accounts.

Primary Software (Required):
Data base management
Word processing

Secondary Software (Optional):
Church finances
Customized

Ministry in Crisis Situations

General comments

Any crisis situation where the pastor must intervene requires a certain amount of accurate information for an effective response. Like the death of a church member, a crisis in the life of a church member places significant emotional stress upon the person or family involved. A crisis situation can result from an automobile accident, a family argument, the arrest of a teenage child for drunk driving, an attempted suicide, or any other stress-causing event.

Suppose the chairwoman of your church's finance committee is seriously injured in an automobile accident. The husband calls you, his frantic voice indicating a desperate panic. Yet, the husband never attends church, while the wife is active in many aspects of the congregation. As the pastor, you know little about the husband and need to find ways in which you can help. You tell him you'll be right over to the hospital. After you hang up the telephone, you turn to the computer and query the data base about the family involved. The computer then gives you important information, including personal counseling data left by the previous pastor. As you walk to your car, a brief look at the data helps you learn a little about the husband and refreshes your memory on some important details about the family. You are grateful for the data because it helps you to react more effectively and personally to the crisis.

Let's change the scenario somewhat. Suppose that none of the family members of the accident victim could be reached, but the police discover a note in the woman's wallet that indicates she is a member of your church. The police call the church hoping to reach someone that can help them locate a family member. You answer the call and hear the distressing news. The authorities need to help locate a family member and to treat the victim. You turn to the computer and receive a printout of medical and family information. The computer has saved many precious moments in the crisis because the information was generated on the screen and printer in less than one minute. In a manual system, gathering the necessary data may have taken five to thirty minutes, which could have meant the difference between life and death for the church member.

One caution: don't be too free in giving information about church members to anyone who asks. You should have prior written permission from the church member to release information, and then you should only give out a member's medical information in an emergency.

A crisis that involves an attempted suicide, depression, loss of a job, family argument, marital conflict, or other personally devastating experience requires certain information in order for you to intervene effectively and relieve the situation. The primary benefit of the computer in a crisis is in providing you with the counseling history of the person and other relevant data.

After the initial crisis has passed, further counseling may be advisable. A data base of local counseling agencies to which a person can be referred may be loaded on a disk. This data can be helpful as you search for the most effective means to help.

Suggested data to be maintained

—All data listed under the "Ministry To the Bereaved" section.

—Medical information on church members including blood type, allergies, brief medical histories, hospital stays that you are aware of, and other useful information. This data, however, should be short and to the point. Only information needed in a medical emergency should be kept. Perhaps consultation with a local physician would help clarify what data is important for your purposes.

—Data on local private and public agencies to which a person can be referred for additional professional counseling. This information might include:

Name of the agency, public or private status
Address and telephone number

Services offered, specialties, e.g., alcoholism
counseling
Names of contact persons at the agency
Cost for services; discount cost scales for
low-income families

Possible reports and other output documents

The reports required in this application will vary
according to the crisis situation you have encountered.
The key in reporting information is to print only that
data essential to your crisis ministry. Generally, time is
of the essence in a crisis, so your reports should be
brief. The exception to this may be in reporting
counseling agency information. In this situation, you
may have the luxury of additional time to provide
referral information to the person being helped
because the immediate crisis has passed.

System comments

This application should be integrated with the
membership data base. Much of the data needed in
crisis situations will be very similar to data used
everyday in normal ministry routines.

The information in this application must be
carefully organized in advance. In other words, it will
save time to know what types of information should be
available at your fingertips if a car accident occurs.
This should be decided PRIOR to actually implementing this application on your computer. If you fail
to systematically organize the crisis information,
MORE time could be spent in using the computer in a
crisis situation than would be used in a manual system.
Thus, the purpose of the system is defeated.

Primary Software (Required):
Data-base management
Report generator

Secondary Software (Optional):
Word processing, depending on the type of reports
   needed
Customized

Birthday and Anniversary Recognition

General comments

Recognizing the birthdays and wedding anniversaries of church members is a common practice among many pastors. It is a nice gesture that reminds church members you are interested in them and the important days in their lives. It tells a church member that you care, and that you're available to help if needed. Birthday and anniversary recognition can provide opportunities for pastoral ministry not previously known to you.

If you manage birthday and anniversary data through a manual system, considerable effort is spent gathering and maintaining the proper information. Such a manual system can be tedious and time-consuming. Indeed, many pastors may not recognize birthdays and anniversaries simply because it takes too much time, and is often mundane administrivia. Even if a secretary is available, an inordinate amount of his or her time can be spent in maintaining birthday and anniversary files.

In a typical manual system, a list is made on a piece of paper that contains the birthdays and anniversaries for church members in a particular month. Then the pastor can respond with a letter, telephone call, or home visit. Regardless of the response, certain information is needed to make the response. For example, if you call the person on the telephone, then you need the telephone number. To obtain the number, you would look it up in the local telephone book or church directory. This consumes more time just for the simple task of recognizing an important day in the life of a church member.

A computer can be of significant assistance in the birthday and anniversary recognition task. For example, instead of pulling the "February Birthday File" from a filing cabinet, you would ask the computer to print the "February Birthday Report." This report would then list not only the name and birthdate of church members in February, but also provide other data crucial to your response, such as the address and telephone number. This automated system would probably save 90 percent of the time needed in a manual system to compile the February birthday list.

Suggested data to be maintained

Name of church member
Address and telephone number
Birthday
Anniversary date, if married
Other important dates in the life of this church member
Church participation history, e.g. committees served on, etc.

Possible reports and other output documents

A birthday or anniversary report would contain the same information as listed in the previous section. It could be listed in the order which best assists you. For example, the report could be listed in ascending birth date order, or it could be printed alphabetically by name. Here is an example of how the headings in such a report might appear:

Birthday	Name	Address	Telephone Number
Current Church Positions	Past Church Positions	Other Data	Pastoral Response

The pastoral response column would be left blank in the printed report so that you can manually record your action with a pen or pencil. A coding system could be devised for this column that might include

L   meaning you sent a letter

C   meaning you sent a card

H   meaning you made a home visit (you could list the date of the visit)

T   meaning you made a telephone call (you could list the date of the call)

Other coding schemes may also work for you, but tracking your response could be helpful later if you are trying to remember just what you did in a certain instance.

At the end of the month, you or your secretary could enter the pastoral responses you made into the computer. Thus, when the next year comes around, you will know exactly what pastoral response you made for the birthday or anniversary the previous year and, if appropriate, avoid using the same type of acknowledgment.

This reporting technique could also be interfaced with the word processing software you have in your computer. If you decide to send a letter as your response to the birthday or anniversary, the church member's name, event date, and other data such as the name of current church position held could be automatically inserted in the body of the letter. The letter could state a simple greeting referring to the person's birthday or anniversary and expressing appreciation for the person's active participation in the church's lay leadership. If the letter is already in the computer all you need to do is ask the machine to move the data from the report into the letter and print it. You would then sign it, seal it, and mail it. At the same time the computer could also record a "L" in the pastoral response column, automatically saving you even more time.

Care should be taken that you do not overload the birthday and anniversary reports with excessive data. Print only that information that is useful to you in birthday or anniversary recognitions.

System comments

This application should be integrated with the membership data base on the computer. All the data items listed above can be easily maintained in a membership data base. The only exception to this would be the pastoral response column. It would probably be necessary to construct a separate computer file for pastoral responses, which is interfaced with the membership data base.

Primary Software (Required):
Data base management
Report generator

Secondary Software (Optional):
Word processing
Customized (may be necessary to accomplish the "pastoral response column" in reports. This will depend on the data base and report generation software.)

Calling

General comments

Part and parcel of the pastoral ministry is visitation or calling. Many pastors enjoy this task, while many others would rather not waste their time with home visitation. Some larger churches consider calling important enough to employ retired pastors as "visitation ministers." Other churches, particularly in rural areas, simply expect the pastor to do the calling. On the other hand, churches in more urban and suburban environments do not expect much calling from the pastor due to the many activities that occupy the church members' attention. In any case, home visitation receives varying levels of emphasis, depending upon the orientation of the congregation and the pastor.

Regardless of how you may personally feel about calling, it is one of the larger, more vital areas of pastoral ministry. Visitation is where much of the bonding between you and your parishioners occurs. It's where you meet them on their "turf," and come to understand the personal environment in which they live.

Hospital visitation is also a large part of the pastoral ministry. Calling upon ill church members gives an emotional boost, which is a significant part of the healing process. Hospital calling also gives you tremendous insight into a church member's life so you can minister to him or her more effectively.

Calling requires a certain amount of organizational administrivia. Information should be maintained and processed in certain ways about each visit so that your calling can become more effective. Manual maintenance of such information is possible in calling, but may not be practical and can be time-consuming. Controlling calling information through a computer adds efficiency to your administrative work, which enables you to have additional time in completing the home visitation expected by your congregation.

Suggested data to be maintained

For all types of calls:

Name of person called

Address and telephone number

Location of call, e.g., home, work, hospital, retirement facility

Calling zone, e.g., Northwest, Southeast, West, etc.

Date of call

Purpose, i.e., general, counseling, illness, death of family member, etc.

General Comments

For home, work place, or retirement facility (in addition to above):

By appointment or surprise?

Was anybody "home?"

Topics discussed, e.g., children, grandchildren, recent activities, health, etc.

General demeanor, e.g., good attitude, depressed, etc.

Follow-up—Is a follow-up needed? What is needed?

For hospital calling:

Reason for hospitalization

Health condition

General demeanor (see above)

Comments of family

Comments of medical personnel

Follow-up

Possible reports and other output documents

Reports in this application would consist of screen information displays about a family to be called on or printed documents that could be maintained in a notebook. Printed documents are primarily used in maintaining a record of your calling.

Screen information displays in hospital calling situations can be used to help prepare you for a hospital visit. For example, having the hospitalization history of a church member can be valuable in helping you understand any chronic difficulties or emotional needs of the member.

System comments

This application is directly dependent upon the membership data base and should be carefully planned or a savings in time will not be achieved. Include only that data which is useful for future reference. The number of data items can always be expanded at a later date, if the currently maintained data proves to be inadequate for your pastoral needs.

The various categories of calling have certain data that is common to each category, while each has its own specific data needs. The relational aspects of the data base software should be used to control the commonality of data between the types of calling.

Primary Software (Required):
Data base management
Secondary Software (Optional):
Customized

Counseling

General comments

Counseling of individual church members is an important part of pastoral ministry. Frequently, a church member will not trust anyone else with the burden of a personal problem other than his or her pastor. This places a great responsibility upon the pastor to provide effective counseling while maintaining the strictest confidentiality.

Many pastors today spend a great amount of time in counseling. A pastor will hear problems in counseling sessions that run the gamut from marital conflict (including extramarital affairs) to personal depression and stress. Trying to maintain records of counseling sessions can be a major administrative headache. Yet, professional counselors feel that adequate notes and records of counseling sessions are very important for future counseling sessions. A counseling history is vital in the treatment of the person because it helps the pastor to know problem areas and suggested remedies previously discussed.

Counseling notes can also help you to keep each counselee separated from others so that you do not become confused. If you are counseling many people at the same time using a mental filing system, it would be easy to remember some obscure point brought up by one counselee that you may unintentionally bring into the counseling session of another. Before each counseling session, a review of the notes from the past several sessions helps refresh your memory and keeps you on target with the particular person being counseled.

Obviously, a manual system can be used to maintain counseling session notes and other related data. However, you could begin to keep a voluminous amount of paper with even just a few counselees. Thus, the computer can be of benefit in helping to organize counseling data into useful formats and reducing paper work.

Suggested data to be maintained

Name of counselee
Address and telephone number

Church member?
Date of last counseling session
Date of next counseling session
General problem, e.g., depression, marital conflict,
etc.
Notes of each session organized by session date
Notes for follow-up in next session

Possible reports and other output documents

Before each counseling session, you could generate
a report that includes the data listed above. Depending
upon your needs, the report might include notes from
all previous counseling sessions, or might only list
notes from the previous one or two sessions. The form
of these reports should be designed to make your
counseling work more effective.

Another output document might include a listing of
private and public agencies that can provide additional
counseling assistance. Often, a pastor may feel that the
counselee's problem is beyond his or her counseling
skills. Thus, a referral may be in order. Refer to the
"Ministry in Crisis Situations" section for additional
information on using a pastoral computer to maintain
data on private and public counseling agencies.

System comments

Counseling data should be interfaced with the
membership data base. Name, address, and telephone
number are pieces of information that should be already
contained in the membership data base. If you are
counseling someone who is not a member of your church,
a separate nonmember data base may be in order. This
will depend entirely upon your pastoral situation.

Confidentiality of counseling information is absolutely
essential. If confidentiality is lacking, your entire
credibility can be destroyed. This is true in a manual

system or automated computer system. If you choose not to use a computer in counseling, then make sure your paper notes are kept under lock and key. If you use a computer, then:

—Protect counseling data through a security system that uses ID and password control or other similar security control measures.

—If you are using floppy disks to store counseling data, keep them under lock and key. In addition, you should keep your counseling disks separate from the disks used for the rest of your work. In this way, if someone deliberately attempts to gain access to your data disks, the counseling disks will be protected with an additional level of security.

—When any report is generated from the computer pertaining to counseling, it should either be kept under lock and key OR destroyed when you are done with it.

Primary Software (Required):

Data base management
Security
Report generator

Secondary Software (Optional):

Word processing, for certain reports or letters that may be exchanged between different counselors working with the same case.
Customized

Premarital Counseling

General comments

Most counseling deals with problems and their possible solutions. However, a subset of counseling that does not deal with specific problems and solutions is premarital or pre-wedding counseling. Indeed, pre-wedding counseling can be fun for the pastor and the couple involved.

Many pastors are very methodical in doing this sort of counseling. Much detailed information must be maintained in order to complete three to five successful sessions of counseling. In addition, many pastors use pre-wedding inventories that deal with personalities, habits, likes, dislikes, and other areas.

Inventories usually require objective responses that lend themselves quite nicely to automation. The computer can record the necessary data of pre-wedding counseling sessions—including inventory responses, scoring, and norm projections. Using the computer in this manner could save administrative time enabling the pastor to spend additional time with the couple as needed.

Suggested data to be maintained

General data for the couple:
> Name of male, address, and telephone number
> Name of female, address, and telephone number
> Ages
> Dates of baptism and church membership status
> Parent's names
> Proposed marriage date
> Dates of counseling sessions

Data for each counseling session:
> Inventories administered
> Topics discussed
> General demeanor of the couple
> Comments
> Follow-up for future sessions

Possible reports and other output documents

Reports in pre-wedding counseling would be similar to reports discussed previously in the counseling section. However, a reference list of private and public agencies that offer pre-wedding counseling services probably does not need to be kept. Pre-wedding counseling is generally between the pastor and couple to be married. Outside counseling services are usually not needed.

System comments

You may or may not need to interface this application with the church's membership data base. That will depend entirely upon your needs. More than likely, a separate pre-wedding data base will need to be created for use in this form of counseling.

As with other types of counseling, confidentiality is absolutely essential. The same suggestions about security as in the counseling section are also applicable in computer-assisted pre-wedding counseling.

Primary Software (Required):
  Data base management
  Security
Secondary Software (Optional):
  Customized

Evangelism

General comments

Discussed heavily in recent years, evangelism is achieved through many ways, with the common goal of bringing more persons to Christ. Evangelism has been the focus of many denominations in recent years, particularly within mainline churches. Many materials have been published about evangelism on both theoretical and practical levels.

This is not a book about evangelism; therefore, it is impossible for me to discuss all the possible evangelistic methodologies and countless materials available. However, this IS a book about information management in the pastoral ministry using computers, and information is required for effective evangelism. Thus, a computer can be used to help control the data needed for an effective evangelistic pastor.

The information required in evangelism will depend directly upon your particular evangelistic emphasis and the needs of your congregation and community. Therefore, this section will discuss briefly three possible evangelism areas that may or may not appeal to you. However, if these areas do not suit you, the ideas brought forth below may give you some help with the particular area emphasized in your ministry.

The three evangelistic areas we shall consider in relationship to information management are:

1. Potential new church members from new persons who just moved into the community or individuals who are long-standing members of the community but are unchurched.
2. Inactive members of your church.
3. Church school.

New persons that have just moved into the community are potential new church members. Data about new folks in the community can be obtained through the public schools, utilities, or community welcome organizations. From the information obtained, an appropriate response such as a visit to the residence, a letter of welcome, a telephone call, or any combination of these can be made.

Potential new church members can also be drawn from those people in your community who are already residents, but not attending any church. These persons may be more difficult to identify than newcomers. You may use a survey to determine who the unchurched are and where they live. The survey can also be administered on a periodic basis to keep you constantly up-to-date on just who the unchurched people are. The computer can maintain this data for easy control and help to select the most appropriate response.

Inactive church members are generally a thorn in the side of most pastors. Inactive church members often insist that they remain members of the church, but refuse to support it in any way. Yet, evangelizing inactive church members can be just as important as evangelizing persons new to the community. While activating an inactive church member may not add numbers to your church rolls, it shows that you are truly interested in the spiritual welfare of all persons, regardless of their church status. If you develop a membership data base, then most, if not all of the data you need about inactive members will already be available through the computer. For example, inactive members can be identified through a worship attendance tracking system. (Attendance tracking is discussed later in this chapter.) After the inactive members have been identified, you can plan and execute the most appropriate response.

The third area of evangelism we shall briefly consider is through the church school. Many recent studies of evangelism have demonstrated that one of the most effective methods of evangelism is through the church school. Growing churches always have thriving church schools. The computer can help here by identifying potential students for the church school through new member lists and inactive member information. The computer can also be used to help identify potential new church members from the student population of the church school. For example, if certain parents who are not members of church are sending their children to your church school, then the computer may be able to identify those parents as potential new church members.

Other evangelistic areas may exist for your ministry and church. Only you and the church's lay leadership can identify what the best evangelistic emphasis is for the congregation. By learning where the community hurts and discovering its needs, plans can be developed for your church to help heal the hurts and fulfill some of the needs. This is evangelism. This is when Christ is served. The computer can help with the what, when, where, who and how so that evangelism planning and execution is more effective.

Suggested data to be maintained

Potential new church members (Persons new to the community):
Name
Address and telephone number
Occupation and employer
Date of arrival in town
Religious preference
Current church membership, if any
Response, e.g., letter, telephone call, call by pastor, call by laity visiting team
Persons living in the community, but unchurched:
Survey data may include items such as why they don't attend church, previous church affiliations (if any), membership in community organizations, and other concerns appropriate to your church.

Other data, if it can be identified either through the survey or by other means:
Name
Address and telephone number
Occupation and employer
Religious preference
Current church membership, if any
Response, e.g., letter, telephone call, call by pastor, call by laity visiting team

Inactive members:
Standard data generated in the membership data base system.
Special information as needed in each particular case. This data will be determined by your particular needs and ministry to inactive church members.

Church School:
Name of student
Address and telephone number
Age
Pre-school, child, youth, adult, senior?
Church school class in which this person is member
Date of baptism
Attendance in church school
Church school teacher of this student
Parents name, address, and telephone number, if student is a child or youth
Comments, e.g., special skills such as playing the piano, learning disability, etc.

Possible reports and other output documents

Reports should be organized in such a way that makes sense for your evangelism emphasis and meets your needs. For example, if you are concentrating on persons in the thirty to forty-five-year-old range, then your reports should be printed by age in that range. Report generating software is a requirement if you wish to develop reports for your specific needs.

By using word processing with automatic document generation, a welcome letter to new persons in the community can already be stored in the computer. The letter can explain the church and its services to the community. It can also offer your assistance as they settle into the community. You simply fill in the blanks with name, address, and other appropriate data as needed.

If you have more than one letter to send, the computer can fill in the necessary blanks in the letter through document generation with your data base. This can save enormous amounts of time; however, the danger in this process is to ignore or forget the person to whom the letters are directed because the computer is doing the administrative work. Thus, you may wish to follow-up the letter with a telephone call or home visit.

Other documents can be produced through the report generator or word processing depending upon your needs. These documents can be useful in any evangelistic emphasis.

System comments

Using the church membership data base is important in the evangelism application. A potential new member data base can be created specifically for evangelism purposes. Then when a person or family recorded in the potential new members data base actually joins the church, their information can be "rolled over" into the regular membership data base.

The rollover technique should be automatic and may require customized software depending upon the data base management software you are using. This technique means that you put a special "flag" in the person's information record that designates when he or she has become a new member. For example, a "0" may mean the person is still a potential member, "1" may mean that the person has joined the church, and "2" may mean that the person will definitely not join the church and should be deleted from the file. When the rollover is executed, then the computer moves all persons with the "1" flag from the potential new member file to the regular membership file and deletes all those persons with a designation of "2." In addition, some provision in the rollover technique should be made to insert the data of membership, how received (profession of faith, transfer, etc.), type of membership (full, adult, youth, preparatory, etc.), and other pertinent data.

Primary Software (Required):
    Data base management
    Report generator
    Word processing
    Customized, if your data base software will not effectively handle a rollover technique

Secondary Software (Optional):
    Customized

Membership and Confirmation Training

General comments

Most churches offer membership and confirmation training for both adults and youth. Membership and confirmation training depends greatly upon your church and denomination. In addition, the pastor usually has the major, if not total responsibility for the training classes. Adult membership training may have class sessions from one to three hours in length with three to twelve sessions in total. Confirmation classes for youth generally last from one to four years with the class meeting each week for one to two hours. Even if the training content varies from one church to another, the *information* needed to effectively manage training classes is similar regardless of denomination.

Using the computer in membership and confirmation training is really a form of Computer Based Education (CBE). CBE can be broken into two major areas: Computer Assisted Instruction (CAI) and Computer Managed Instruction (CMI). CAI is where the student directly uses the computer in the learning process. CMI, on the other hand, is where the teacher uses the computer as an aid to help maintain the many details of each student such as grades, attendance, etc. Both CAI and CMI can be used in membership and confirmation training classes; however, CAI is not discussed in this book any further and CMI in membership and confirmation training classes is only briefly considered. If you wish to have further information on CBE, I suggest you refer to *Computer-Assisted Instruction: A Book of Readings* (Atkinson and Wilson), *Selecting the Church Computer* (William R. Johnson), or other books that discuss it in more detail.

Suggested data to be maintained

CMI information in an adult membership training class:

Name of student
Address and telephone number
Age
Occupation and employer
Date of baptism
Type of proposed membership, e.g., transfer, profession of faith, full, probationary, etc.
Sessions completed
Materials used

CMI information in a confirmation training class:

All data listed for adult membership class should be included

Class attendance records

Tests taken

Memory work completed

Assignments completed

Other information as needed

Possible reports and other output documents

Reports for training classes would include information that enables student progress tracking. The reports should probably be generated prior to each class session. They could be kept in a notebook that might become a "gradebook." Training class reports should also be flexible in format so the information can be organized in the ways that best fulfill your CMI needs. Such flexibility requires report generating software.

System comments

Some interface with the membership data base is required. This eliminates duplication of entries in the future. In addition, using the rollover technique is recommended with this application. The rollover method will probably require customized software. See the section on evangelism in this chapter for further information on rollovers.

Primary Software (Required):

Data base management

Customized, if rollover is not available in the data base software

Secondary Software (Optional):

None suggested. Secondary software will depend upon needs.

Sunday Worship Attendance Records

General Comments

Attendance at Sunday worship is one of the most revealing indicators of a true commitment to the work and life of the church. Trying to understand the attendance patterns of selected church members is also a way to become a more effective pastor/shepherd. For example, if a certain church member or family has been faithful in attendance and then suddenly stops coming to worship, something must be wrong. If a certain member or family never attends worship, but insist that they remain members of the congregation, then something is definitely wrong. If a certain family or person that has never attended worship suddenly begins faithful attendance, something must be right and that "something" should be investigated as a potential method of evangelism.

The pastor should be concerned when certain identifiable patterns appear in worship attendance so that a proper pastoral response can be made. This response will probably be a home visit, but may also be a letter or telephone call. In any case, it is important for you to know what event has prompted an individual or family to stop or start regular attendance at Sunday worship.

In a small church, it is much easier to use a manual system to track attendance patterns. In a church where the average worship attendance is about fifty persons, you can simply observe that the Jones family has missed worship three Sundays in a row where they were faithful attendees previously. A response can then be initiated. In other words, it may not be worth the effort to use a computer in worship attendance tracking in a small church. Only you can decide if this application is worth the benefits received.

Even in a small church, however, attendance tracking can be helpful in maintaining records to calculate the average worship attendance for a season or year. This information can then be rolled over into any judicatory reports that require a listing of average attendance.

If your average worship attendance is large, making it difficult to observe individual and family worship patterns, then the computer can be of immense benefit. Each week the names of persons who attend worship can be entered into the computer. At this point, a report is printed of those persons who have missed, for example, more than three Sundays in a row when they very seldom missed before. The report is then used to initiate the appropriate pastoral response and/or given to a lay calling team in the church.

Regardless of church size, attendance records in general can be very useful in planning. The computer can maintain congregational attendance patterns, which can then be projected into the future for designing budgets, programs, building needs, and so forth. Using spreadsheet software, the attendance numbers can be plugged into standard projection formulas for more effective planning.

Suggested data to be maintained

Name of person or family
Address and telephone number
Date of Sunday worship
Offering given (optional: should be interfaced with the pledge accounting system in the church's computer if one is available)
Pastoral call desired?

Possible reports and other output documents

Reports in this application will vary with your particular needs. For example, as mentioned previously, a report that lists all persons and families who have missed three or more Sundays could be produced. Another example is a report that lists all persons and families who have missed five Sundays out of the last ten.

Another possible report that can be generated from this application is a listing of all those persons who checked the box on the attendance form that desire a pastoral call. This list can then assist you in planning your calling for the week.

Other output documents in this application may include a standard reminder letter sent to the person or family whose name has appeared on the "missing" list. For example, you might consider six missed Sundays as needing a home visit to determine what is wrong, but three missed Sundays are a danger signal that only needs a letter. The computer could choose all those persons from the report file that have missed three Sundays and automatically insert their names and addresses into a standard "we've missed you" letter.

Another possible report is a listing of church members who suddenly begin to attend Sunday worship where they failed to do so previously. This report can help a pastor in two ways:

1. By calling on the family or individual, the pastor may be able to determine what event has prompted their attendance. This could be a new way to reach inactive church members or unchurched persons.
2. The event could be a crisis or problem where the appropriate pastoral response can be initiated.

Report generation software for this application would be helpful in organizing the reports in ways that are useful to you. For example, you simply might want an alphabetical listing by name, or you might want a two-level sort with an alphabetical listing by name within groups by the number of Sundays of missed. A report generator is essential for this task.

Sample headings of a report in this application might be:

Name	Address	Telephone Number	Number of Sundays Missed
Attendance Patterns	Pastoral Response	Family Response	

After the report is generated, you could record both your response and the family's response to your inquiry. This record could be very useful in the future when attempting to analyze attendance patterns for evangelistic purposes.

System comments

Attendance tracking should be interfaced with the membership data base system. When tracking worship attendance, the information in the membership data base can help you determine why a person or family has failed to attend church and help you plan a response.

If you record the family's actions in the computer when you have inquired about their absence, then confidentiality is also vitally important. The same sugestions about security discussed in the section on couneling also apply to this situation.

Primary Software (Required):
Data base management
Word processing
Report generator
Secondary Software (Optional):
Spreadsheet
Customized

10

Worship Computer Applications

God is spirit, and those who worship him must worship in spirit and truth.

John 4:24

One of the major responsibilities of any pastor is in the leadership of worship. Worship in the life of a majority of church members is the only contact they have with the church. Thus, the impression of the weekly worship experience on a church member can make the difference between the member's true Christian commitment and becoming an inactive, apathetic member. Thus, this dichotomy between member commitment and apathy requires the pastor to present a consistent, meaningful worship experience each week.

Worship in almost all modern churches occurs every Sunday throughout the year. In addition, formal worship services frequently occur on weekdays in some churches. If proper worship planning is done, a pastor will spend a large amount of time preparing an effective Sunday worship experience. In churches where several worship services are offered each Sunday or where weekday worship is a regular occurrence, the pastor needs to work even harder. Keeping track of what worship resources have been used and when can become a time-consuming, tedious task that keeps a pastor from making his or her appointed rounds.

The computer can help in several ways with maintaining worship records and in preparing the weekly order of worship. This chapter discusses two primary worship computer applications:

—Worship Resource Control

—Sunday Bulletin Preparation

The primary aim of worship computer applications is to help in the maintenance of needed administrative records so that efficient tracking of what items have been used is possible.

Worship Resource Control

General comments

A worship resource is some liturgical item used in the worship experience other than the sermon. Worship resources include prayers, hymns, calls to worship, and other items used in worship. Such resources are used to make the worship experience more meaningful for the worshipers.

Frequently, worship resources are chosen to follow a theme that may or may not be tied in with the sermon. This theme may be related to the current lectionary readings, denominational lections, or could be a subject of the pastor's own choosing.

Many pastors consistently use suggested worship resources available in a myriad of printed materials. Such materials include books, subscription services, and journals. Other worship resources that a pastor might use include religious poems, devotional readings, illustrations, hymns, songs, etc.

If you don't keep records of when these resources have been used, repetitiveness becomes a real danger. A worship experience can become deadly dull if the church members detect excessive repetition from Sunday to Sunday. Certainly, some items should be repeated every Sunday such as The Lord's Prayer and other liturgies that may be required by your denomination. However, in items where the pastor has freedom of choice, it is easy to forget what has been used before.

A manual system to track the usage of worship resource is an adequate method. However, an automated system is better. A manual system can be invented by each pastor to meet his or her needs, but may become cumbersome. An automated system can be easy, helpful, and a time saver. For example, in an automated system, the computer can maintain a list of hymns used in worship. Figure 10-1 contains an example of such a hymn list.

Figure 10-1

Hymns Used in Worship

Date Used	Hymn #	Hymn #2	Hymn #3
3/4/84	250	433	194
3/11/84	25	366	365
3/18/84	157	264	92
3/25/84	1	128	464

A hymn list like the one in Figure 10-1 provides a helpful way of remembering so that the same hymn isn't used more than two or three times a year. When planning for the next Sunday's worship, the computer can search the list of hymns already used in worship checking the proposed hymns for next Sunday to see if they have been used recently. A manual system could also maintain a list like the one above, but the search can be completed more quickly and easily by a computer.

Suggested data to be maintained

For all items except hymns:

Item classification, e.g., prayer, etc.

Item number

Date used

Liturgical season, e.g., Advent, Lent, Pentecost

Physical location of item, e.g., file folder name, book of worship, etc.

Description and/or comments, e.g., contributed by Mr. and Mrs. James Roberts; borrowed from St. Paul's Feb. newsletter, etc.

Other items to include will depend upon needs, for example, author, topic

For hymns and songs:

Date used

Hymn or song number

Hymnal, for those churches who use more than one hymnal or songbook

Comments, e.g., special song written and sung by John Miles

Possible reports and other output documents

Reports and output documents in this application are basically data base queries where the computer is asked if and when a certain item has been used. The query can be used to provide all related data about an item, the most recent date used, or any combination of needed information. Reports can go to the computer screen unless you require a printed copy. Printed reports can be placed in a file folder, three-ring notebook, or other storage device.

In the case of hymns and songs, the query is primarily aimed at the dates used. The query could ask whether or not a hymn has been used in the last twelve, six, or three months. If it has, then the dates can be listed on the screen.

Report headings should be placed in the way that best suits your needs. For example, the report can be printed in chronological order by date used or it can be printed by item number. A report generator is needed to create reports and output documents.

System comments

Worship resources such as prayers, poems, readings and calls to worship would have to be organized into a numbering system, unless these items are already numbered in their original source. Careful thought should be given to such a numbering system BEFORE the computer is used in worship resource control. This is because you will be using both the computer and physical locations (files, books, etc.) to retrieve and maintain the resources. The numbering system should be organized to reflect an automated approach to worship resource control, as well as the physical retrieval of the items.

Whether or not the actual resource text should be entered into the computer is debatable. Typing each and every prayer, joke, and poem into the computer will take enormous amounts of time and consume large amounts of disk storage. An automated *reference* system is probably much better than storing the actual resources in the computer. Eventually, denominational publishing houses may offer subscription services, whereby worship resources are sent to a pastor on floppy disks or can be downloaded into a pastoral computer from large data bases accessed through communications. However, until such services are available—storage, time, and cost limitations strongly suggest that a reference system for worship resources is much more practical.

Primary Software (Required):
Data base management
Report generator
Secondary Software (Optional):
Customized

Sunday Bulletin Preparation

General comments

One of the most famous landmarks of the modern church is the Sunday bulletin. Almost every church has a Sunday bulletin, which usually contains the order of worship and announcements of church and community importance. Church bulletins serve as a method of communication in the community of faith and assist in focusing the worship experience for participants.

Bulletins contain certain information and words that are repeated each week. Retyping static bulletin information each week takes time. Whether you or your secretary does the actual typing, a poor use of both the secretary's and your time is the result.

Word processing can help you prepare the Sunday bulletin. It becomes a relatively simple matter to insert the necessary items for a Sunday into a generic bulletin stored on a disk and then print it for duplication.

Suggested data to be maintained

The data to be maintained for a generic bulletin depends entirely upon your pastoral situation. Figure 10-2 contains an example of an actual generic order of worship that can be stored in a computer's word processing system. The blanks in this generic bulletin would be filled in each week as the worship preparations are made.

Figure 10-2

Generic Sunday Bulletin Stored in a Computer

St. Matthew's Community Church
(Date), 10:00 A.M.

General Ministers: All Members
Music Minister: Ann P. Jacobs
Pastoral Minister: Mark F. Richards

*   *   *   *   *   *   *   *   *   *   *   *   *   *   *

Enter to Worship . . .
Prelude and Personal Meditation
Call to Worship (L = Leader, C = Community)
   L: C:
   L: C:
*Hymn #   :
Invocation
   L: The Lord be with you.
   C: And also with you.
   L: Let us pray together
   All:
Prayer of Confession
Responsive Reading #   , page
*The Gloria Patri
Anthem
Children's Message
Informal Moments
The Scripture Lessons
Sermon
*Hymn #   :
Community Prayers and the Lord's Prayer
The Offertory
*Hymn #   :
*Benediction
*Postlude
*Leave to Serve . . .
   *The community will please stand

*   *   *   *   *   *   *   *   *   *   *   *   *   *   *

(Announcements go here)

Possible reports and other output documents

The obvious output document from this application is the Sunday bulletin. The procedure to follow is to copy the generic bulletin into another word processing document, insert the appropriate data, and print the completed bulletin.

The reason for copying the generic bulletin is if you fill in the blanks on your generic copy, it is no longer generic! You would then have to create another generic bulletin in the computer, which means retyping the static information. This defeats the purpose of using the computer for bulletin production. You could also simply type over last week's data in creating the new bulletin through the word processing system; however, this does not provide enough flexibility in allowing for special one time only Sunday events.

If you want to cut a stencil of your bulletin, then it is recommended that a letter quality printer be used. Letter quality printers have the best possible stencil cutting capabilities of all types of computer printers. An *impact* dot matrix printer can be used for cutting stencils, but may be frustrating depending upon the type of printer. Some problems have been reported by pastors who are using a dot matrix printer to cut stencils. It is also important to note that a nonimpact printer (e.g., ink jet or laser) will not cut a stencil. If you do not want to try cutting stencils on your computer's printer, then you can print the bulletin on regular paper and use an electronic stencil cutter if you have one to create the bulletin stencil. If you do not have an electronic stencil cutter or printer that will cut stencils, the computer can still be used to produce a Sunday bulletin. After creating the bulletin in the computer, then you print a copy and simply type an original stencil in a regular typewriter, using the computer printed bulletin as a rough draft guide.

System comments

Depending upon your needs, it may be useful to store bulletins of previous Sundays on a disk. However, electronic storage of bulletins is not recommended if disk storage is a problem. The electronic storage of Sunday bulletins will use substantial amounts of disk space over a period of time, which costs additional money. It is less costly and easier to store a copy of each week's bulletin in a file folder. However, if cost is not a factor for you, then the electronic storage of bulletins may be appropriate.

Primary Software (Required):

Word processing

Secondary Software (Optional):

None

11

Sermon Computer Applications

Seeing the crowds, he went up on the mountain. . . . And he opened his mouth and taught them.

Matthew 5:1-2

The preaching of sermons is as ancient as the Scriptures. Forceful and inspiring sermons have enthralled thousands of listeners and led multitudes to Christ and his teachings. Preaching is probably the single most important visible activity of a pastor, having the potential to affect more people in a fifteen to thirty minute period each week than all other pastoral efforts and activities combined.

Interpreting the Scriptures and preaching the Word is a sacred trust. Thus, it should be approached with a sacred and serious attitude. Effective preaching requires the disciplines of study and research, coupled with abiding faith and grace. Sermon preparation requires time spent each day so that the Word is interpreted correctly and that Christ is made real to the hearers.

Each pastor has his or her own style of preaching. Some techniques include using a simple outline, an extended outline, a manuscript, or preaching extemporaneously. Regardless of the technique, the end result is the same—preaching the Word. However, for the end result to be achieved, several steps need to be taken to make preaching effective.

Sermon preparation and storage can be outlined as follows. The steps marked with an asterisk indicate those that can be assisted by a computer.

Prayer and devotion for guidance
Scripture selection
*Research on the Scripture selection (commentaries,
    concordance, study Greek and/or Hebrew trans-
    lations, etc.)
*Outline sermon
*Choose possible illustrations
*Write, edit, and type sermon as many times as needed
*Classify sermon
Practice
Preach
*Store classification data and file sermon

Research

General comments

An important initial step in developing a sermon is biblical and historical research. The purpose of research is to understand what the Scripture means in its proper context. If done properly, research provides a method of exegesis rather than isogesis. Research helps the pastor determine what was being said by the Scripture to the people of biblical times and what is being said to the people of current times. Through research, the pastor can determine the intended meaning of the Scripture passage he or she has chosen for the sermon.

Many excellent biblical and historical research tools are available for sermon development. Some of them include Greek and Hebrew Bibles, Bible dictionaries, concordances, commentaries, and study guides. All of these might be used in the process of developing a particular sermon or only one may be needed, depending upon the sermon.

A computer can help use research tools efficiently. Dictionaries, concordances, and commentaries lend themselves well to automation because of their highly organized nature. For example, consider a computerized concordance. Suppose you need to determine all the occurrences of the word *grace* in the gospel of John. Enter *grace* into the computer concordance and after a search is completed, the machine produces a list of all Scripture sentences in which the word *grace* occurs. The automated Bible dictionary functions in a similar fashion. The simple entry of a word into the computer's Bible dictionary can display or print the word's interpretation. In both of these examples, time is saved because you don't have to pour over difficult-to-read, eye-straining volumes. You can be preparing other items related to the sermon while the computer performs the tedious, repetitive aspects of research.

Suggested data to be maintained

The data to be maintained is directly dependent upon which research tool is being used. In a more general sense, however, the following items probably should be maintained:

Scriptures
Bible words
Related pieces, e.g., a poem or hymn that comments on a certain Scripture passage.

Possible reports and other output documents

Reports consist primarily of query results that can be displayed on the computer's screen. The item to be researched is entered, the result of the query is displayed on the screen, and the screen can then be printed if a "hardcopy" is needed.

Reports could also be transferred to a temporary disk file if the actual text of the item is stored on a disk. Perhaps you have found some item that you would like to quote in your sermon. Storing the item in a temporary file for later use and then moving it into your sermon at the appropriate place saves time because the item does not have to be directly typed into the sermon text.

System Comments

Sermon research data can consume enormous amounts of disk space. Using a concordance or dictionary search will be slow in a micro-computer and especially slow when using floppy disks. The time it takes the computer to search for a requested item may be more than it would have taken you to look it up manually in the first place! Use your common sense for this application so that the primary purpose of saving time is not defeated.

The entry of all the research data could be done personally by you or it could also be done by your secretary. However, entering a Bible concordance, dictionary, or other research tool into your computer takes a long time. Some software vendors have concordances and Bible dictionaries already available for computers, and other automated sermon research tools will probably appear in the future. It is recommended that you purchase the software and sermon research data from a vendor, so you don't have to do the entry yourself.

Interfacing is needed with word processing, so quotations and other research data can be easily transferred into the sermon text.

Primary Software (Required):
Customized software is best for this application so you don't have to do the initial entry work. Check

to make sure that integration between the customized software and the computer's word processing software is possible.

Secondary Software (Optional):
Word processing
Data base

Outline Development

General comments

Sermon outline development is a time-consuming, intensely creative process. From my personal experience, I find that when the outline is completed, about 50 percent to 70 percent of the sermon development work is done, particularly if a manuscript is to be written from the outline.

Using the computer in sermon outlining is primarily a word processing function. The computer will allow you to easily create and edit a sermon outline that follows your needs.

Suggested data to be maintained

Selected Scripture
Main points of the sermon
Sub-points
Suggested hymns and songs
Sermon topic
Sermon title

Possible reports and other output documents

After the outline is entered into the computer, it can be displayed on the screen or printed on the printer in its entirety. If the outline is printed, it can be used as the source document to preach from or it can be used as a guide in writing the sermon manuscript.

A possible format for a printed outline document is:
>Title
>Scripture reference
>Topic(s)
>Suggested hymns and songs
>**Actual outline:**
>Introduction
>Point A (with suggested illustration numbers)
>>Sub-points
>
>Point B (with suggested illustration numbers)
>>Sub-points
>
>Point C (with suggested illustration numbers)
>>Sub-points
>
>Conclusion

System comments

As the sermon outline is developed, a windowing technique can be very helpful. The research data and illustration data can be in two separate windows while the outline is in the primary window. Having all your sermon data in front of you on the computer's screen can be of great help in developing a better sermon outline. Refer to chapter 4 for a further discussion of windows.

Primary Software (Required):
>Word processing
>Some off-the-shelf generic outline software is also available. If you choose to use generic outline software, check on its level of integration with the word processing software.

Secondary Software (Optional):
>Data base, if trying to use a multiple windowing technique in this application.

Illustrations

General comments

Sermon illustrations are useful vehicles to emphasize the important points of a sermon to everyday experiences. Skillfully using illustrations helps your congregation identify closely with the sermon message.

The primary use of a pastoral computer for sermon illustrations is in the storage and retrieval of reference data about illustrations and possibly even the illustration text. For example, the computer can present you with a list of illustrations on a specified topic. If any of the illustrations has been used before, the computer can give the previous date of use. Once an illustration has been selected, it can be transferred to a temporary sermon writing file if the illustration text has been stored electronically and moved into the sermon text at the appropriate time.

Evenutally, electronic publishers in the religious field will offer sermon illustrations on floppy disks. Thus, you would be able to load those illustrations into the computer without rekeying every one. However, you may also wish to keep your illustrations on paper in file folders and only use the computer for illustration reference purposes.

Suggested data to be maintained

Type of illustration, e.g., poem, joke, story
Date used, if any
Sermon title the illustration was used in, if any
Topic(s), e.g., discipleship, resurrection, tithing, stewardship
Physical file location
Actual text of the illustration, if appropriate
Scripture reference of illustration, if appropriate

Possible reports and other output documents

A report in this application might consist of a list of all illustrations under a certain topic. First, the topic name would be entered into the computer. The computer then searches for all illustrations and their reference data under this topic and prepares a computer file containing them. After the search, the selected illustrations can be displayed or printed. The illustrations needed for the sermon can then be selected and moved into a temporary word processing file for insertion into the sermon text at a later time.

System comments

Interface between the illustration data base and word processing is needed in this application. Also, if you plan to purchase illustrations from a publisher, make sure that an interface with your computer's data base and word processing software is possible.

The temporary file should be deleted after the sermon is completed. However, be sure to record the date used for the selected illustrations in the permanent illustration file.

Primary Software (Required):
Data base
Word processing, if data base and word processing
are integrated
Secondary Software (Optional):
Customized

Writing, Editing, and Printing

General comments

After the research has been completed, the outline written, and the illustrations selected, the actual writing of the manuscript begins. Formulating the manuscript is a creative process that follows the original thinking developed in the outline.

Once a first draft of the manuscript is written, editing is necessary to make the manuscript stronger, more coherent, and have a smoother flow. Several drafts of the manuscript may be written before it is satisfactory. Finally, with the sermon manuscript in its completed form, the printer produces the document that can be taken into the pulpit.

Sermon writing is usually done by hand with pen or pencil, or by typewriter. However, through word processing, the computer can now be used exclusively in the writing, editing, and printing of the sermon manuscript. The flowchart in Figure 11-1 illustrates the process of producing the final copy of the sermon manuscript. (A *flowchart* is a diagram that shows how each action in a system relates to the others. The symbols used in the flowchart in Figure 11-1 are the actual symbols used by computer programmers in developing a flowchart.)

Suggested data to be maintained

Temporary files with quotes and illustrations
Outline

Possible reports and other output documents

After entering the sermon manuscript, it can be printed whenever you need a hardcopy. The output can be either a draft copy for editing purposes or final copy for use in the pulpit depending upon needs. It may be helpful if the final copy is printed in pica type or even orator type (larger than pica). For ease of reading in the pulpit, the larger type is preferable. Double spacing should also be used for easier editing and reading.

Figure 11-1

SERMON DEVELOPMENT FLOWCHART

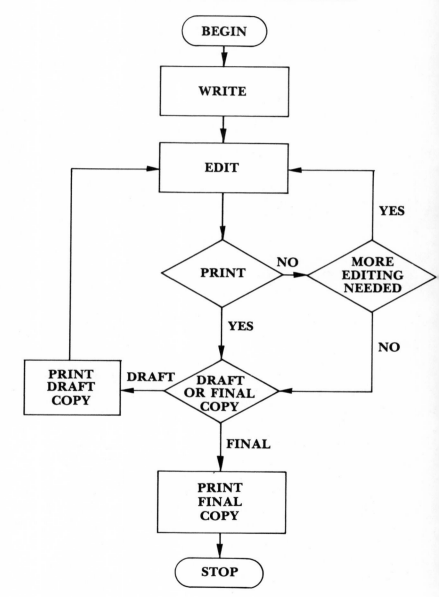

System comments

A systematic approach in writing, editing, and printing a sermon manuscript means you are receiving maximum use of your computer. Developing a systematic method in this application will probably create a more effective sermon and help your overall pastoral information system to be more efficient.

Primary Software (Required):

Word Processing

Secondary Software (Optional):

None

Storage and Retrieval

General Comments

There are two types of storage related to sermons:

1. Data about sermons
2. The actual outlines and/or manuscripts

Many pastors maintain certain information about their sermons manually. This information is kept in card files, notebooks, journals, and other printed media. The primary purpose of storing data about sermons is to provide a sermon reference system and to maintain a record of all sermons preached. The data often includes items such as sermon title, Scripture, and when and where preached.

Sermon reference information can be organized in a variety of ways. For example, it is kept by title, by topics, by Scripture, in chronological order, or in any combination of these. The computer lends itself particularly well to this type of organization through data base formats.

Most pastors also store their sermon outlines and manuscripts in some type of file folder or notebook. Some type of reference number or Scripture referencing system is generally used when storing sermons so that easy retrieval is possible.

If the outline and manuscript is developed on the computer, then it can be stored electronically for future use. After all, once it has been created through the computer, it can be left on a floppy disk for future use if you have sufficient disk space. Sermon outlines and manuscripts can also be printed and then stored in file folders, notebooks, or whatever method is most appropriate. The physical storage of sermons serves as a backup if a disk develops errors or if disk space is a problem on your computer.

Pastors who have been preaching for several years wonder about loading all previously preached sermons onto a disk for electronic storage. This can be done but would require substantial work if each sermon must be typed into the word processing system.

An alternative to typing every old sermon into the computer is to use an Optical Character Recognition (OCR) device. An OCR device is a piece of hardware that works together with specialized software to read text from a printed page and store it in the computer. OCR devices save many hours of time because they can read typed text much faster than it can be typed. OCR machines have existed for many years on large computers and are beginning to appear in the micro-computer market.

It is possible to purchase an OCR device with software for a micro-computer and load your old sermons onto a disk. However, consider the real value of storing old sermons electronically before proceeding with this plan because additional expense will be involved. Also, the time required to use an OCR device for sermon entry could be prohibitive, depending upon the number of sermons you have. In addition, once the OCR device has been used for the old sermons, what else will it be used for? In other words, you must decide if the cost of such a device is worth the benefit of having your old sermons stored electronically through your computer. If you want to use an old sermon, then perhaps entering only the sermon you want for editing purposes at the time you need it is more appropriate than storing all your old sermons.

Suggested data to be maintained

Sermon title
Scripture text reference of sermon
Topic(s)
Liturgical season, e.g., Pentecost, Advent, etc.
Special days, e.g., Easter, Christmas Day, etc.
Suggested hymns and songs that go with the sermon
Two or three sentence description
Date(s) and location(s) of preaching this sermon
Physical file location

Possible reports and other output documents

Reports can be generated in a variety of formats, and they can either be displayed on the computer's screen or printed on the printer. There are several ways in which reports containing sermon data can be generated:

1. Title searches
2. Topical searches
3. Scriptural searches
4. Title listings
5. Chronological listings by date of preaching
6. Printing of electronically stored sermons for retrieval, editing, and preaching again.

A report generator is essential in this application to produce the types of reports needed. After the report documents have been printed, they can be physcially stored in notebooks or file folders depending upon needs.

System comments

If you decide to investigate the OCR option for loading old sermons, make sure the OCR device is compatible with your computer AND word processing software. A thorough investigation of the OCR device is recommended in order to reduce unwanted and frustrating surprises.

Integration between the data base of sermon information and word processing can be helpful. For example, after a sermon has been located through the data base, then moving immediately to word processing would enable the editing and printing of the sermon without extra steps.

Primary Software (Required):
Data base
Report generator
Word processing
Secondary Software (Optional):
Customized

12

Administrative Computer Applications

Now there are varieties of gifts, but the same Spirit; and there are varieties of service, but the same Lord; and there are varieties of working, but it is the same God who inspires them all in every one.

I Corinthians 12:4-6

Administrative computer applications in the pastoral ministry are those tasks that require the maintenance of minute details for organizational purposes. The information maintained in administrative areas provides indirect, qualitative benefits for ministry. In other words, the computer saves time in controlling the many details necessary for the pastoral ministry by creating additional time for working directly with the members of the congregation.

Pastoral ministry administrative computer applications discussed in this chapter include:

—General Correspondence and Reports
—Mass Mailings and Repetitive Reports
—Pastoral Records
—Name and Address Lists
—Newsletter Processing and Production
—Interests, Talents, and Skills Inventory
—Church Financial Planning
—Personal Finance
—Tickler Files
—Judicatory Reports

Some administrative computer applications suggested in this chapter overlap with fuctions that might be done by church staff or volunteers other than the pastor. However, in smaller churches the pastor is often directly responsible for the church's administrivia described in each of these applications.

General Correspondence and Reports

General Comments

Every pastor has letters, reports, and other documents that require either handwriting or typing. Letters can range from a letter written for a specific purpose to the completion of a form letter for baptismal or genealogical verifications. Reports may consist of a single page description of your monthly activities for the church board to a lengthy report of your recommendations concerning evangelism in your church. Other documents may contain text or numerical information that should be kept for future reference or provided to a particular committee.

The computer can be of significant benefit in producing such documents. For example, when you receive a baptism verification request that is needed for Social Security purposes, standard paragraphs for this purpose can already be in the computer. All you need to do is fill in the blanks by completing the name, date of baptism, and officiating pastor, whereupon a complete letter is printed. Obviously, considerable time is saved because the standard, repeatable paragraphs are already in the computer.

This application suggests using a letter quality printer. Many persons today react negatively to a dot matrix printed letter. As discussed in chapter 5, people frequently refer to such documents in a derogatory way—"computer letters." Computer letters are often ignored because the person harbors a feeling that the computer has written the letter. Yet, dot matrix printers are less expensive than letter quality printers. Thus, your choice of printers is weighed in the balance of economy versus quality. Is it more important to save money or have better quality output? To answer this question, you must know the persons to whom correspondence will be sent or the groups for whom reports need to be provided. If your audience has a wide mixture of preferences, then I recommend the conservative approach: a letter quality printer. On the other hand, after consultation with the appropriate persons, you may discover a dot matrix printer is sufficient. If you can afford it *and if your computer can support it,* then you may opt to have both dot matrix and letter quality printers as output devices.

Suggested data to be maintained

The data to be maintained in this application is paradoxically nothing and everything! There is no specific data to be maintained because the information needed for letters and reports is available through the membership data base and other files discussed previously. On the other hand, all information already being maintained in other files will be used in your correspondence and reports. Thus, nothing and everything is needed, depending entirely upon your needs and the types of documents you will produce through this application.

However, certain textual information will need to be kept in a more general sense. Standard paragraphs and phrases that you would use in a letter or report should be entered and retrieved as needed. For example, a form letter for baptism verification can be maintained in the computer and when a verification request is made, you simply fill in the blanks. The textual information you maintain will be directly dependent upon your needs.

Possible reports and other output documents

Unlike other applications, there are no standard reports in this area. The output produced from this application would be word processing documents that use the printing routines supplied with your word processing software. These documents can only be planned for as each specific letter or report is needed.

If possible, you should use regular church or personal stationary when generating letters. If your printer has pressure feed or a cut-sheet feeder, then single sheets from regular paper stocks can be used. (A pressure-feed printer is like a typewriter. It uses friction to hold your paper in place while the printing is done. A cut-sheet feeder is a piece of hardware that automatically feeds single sheets of paper into a pressure-feed printer.) If your printer has only a pin or tractor feed requiring paper with holes on the sides, then you will need to have a paper supplier print your stationary with perforated holes so you can use your printer. (A printer with a pin or tractor feed uses a mechanical device to pull the paper through the printer.)

Regular bond paper is more than sufficient for the printing of reports. You can use either single sheets, fan fold, or perforated hole paper, depending upon your printer and its accessories.

You should be aware of one major caution in this application. It is possible to waste large amounts of paper when printing letters and reports. Because it is so easy to change a word or phrase, you can edit, print a copy, change another word, and print another copy. When using a regular typewriter, changes are more difficult to make because it means retyping the entire document. Thus, careful planning is necessary so that paper waste is kept to a minimum when using a computer. Paper and printer ribbons are expensive and adequate planning will help to keep these long-term costs lower.

System comments

This application may be interfaced with data base and spreadsheet software through the windows technique. Several generic software packages are available that integrate the data base, spreadsheet, and word processing functions. Such integration allows considerable flexibility in creating and editing information between applications. See chapter 4 for more information on integrated software using windows.

If you use customized software for the maintenance of your data bases, then integrating word processing software with your programs may be difficult. Careful analysis is needed at this point because such an interface is extremely beneficial to overall system planning and efficiency.

Be careful to delete unused and unnecessary letter and document files. There is a tendency in computer work to create files and forget about them when you no longer need them. However, even if you don't need a file after it has been used, the file is still consuming storage space on the disk. Storing inactive files on active disks is inefficient and will cause computer degradation. (Degradation reduces the efficiency of the computer's internal operations.) Thus, on a periodic basis, either delete inactive files or copy them to "inactive" back-up or archival disks, if they may be needed sometime in the future.

Primary Software (Required):
Word processing

Secondary Software (Optional):
  Data base
  Spreadsheet
  Customized

Mass Mailings and Repetitive Reports

General comments

Sometimes a pastor finds it necessary to send a letter or report to every member of the congregation. For example, such a mass mailing might be a letter promoting the new church fund drive, an announcement of a special worship service, or the publication of some community event. Yet, the pastor may feel that "Dear Friend," "Dear Church Member," or some other general salutation are not adequate for the mailing. A personalized letter with individual salutations is better, while retaining the key standard paragraphs that should be sent to all church members.

When a manual system is used to personalize a mass mailing, each letter or document is typed individually in its entirety. If you have twenty letters, then twenty original documents must be typed containing the same paragraphs but with different names, addresses, and salutations. This is a tedious and time-consuming task for either you or your secretary. If you have two hundred letters to type, you'll feel frustrated because the amount of time needed to complete all the letters seems wasteful and unproductive. If you have two thousand letters to type, then you would probably throw up your hands and go to a less personal approach.

A computer can be of immense value in mass document production that you wish to personalize. The letter or document needs to be typed only once, and after the necessary name, address, and salutatation files for the document have been set up, the computer prints an individualized letter for each church or family, with a personalized name, address, and salutation to suit your needs. Because the letter is entered only once into the computer and the machine does the printing for you, massive amounts of time are saved and personalization is achieved.

This document generation method can also be used to produce monthly financial reports, membership statistics, and other important reports of a repetitive nature. Each time the document is to be printed, the computer will retrieve any information specified by you from the data base and insert it into the body of the document.

Suggested data to be maintained
   For letters:
      Name
      Address
      Preferred salutation
      Other specific data as your needs require. This data can probably come from the membership data base.

Possible reports and other output documents

Letters produced through a document generation process will follow the same format as normal correspondence. When entering the letter into the computer, include variables for each piece of data to be inserted. (A variable is a piece of information that changes with each document produced.) The variable goes where you want the item to appear in the letter. Following are two examples of this. The variables are offset by an asterisk.

   1. A pastoral letter can be sent to all church members whose pledges are paid and up-to-date, congratulating them for their faithful support.

The name, address, and salutation data would probably come from the membership data base and the pledge amount from the financial data base:

Date of letter
* Name of person or family *
* Address of person or family *
* City, state, and zip code *

Dear * Salutation * :
    I would like to thank you personally for your continued faithful support of our church's ministry. Your pledge of * Amount of pledge * is currently paid and up to date. Without your support and the support of others like you, our church's ministry would be in serious jeopardy.

Sincerely yours,

2. A letter could be sent to all church members who have failed to pay their pledge during the last three months:

Date of letter
* Name of person or family *
* Address of person or family *
* City, state, and zip code *

Dear * Salutation * :
    I'm sure you would agree that our church's ministry is a vital asset to this community. However, like any other endeavor, the church's ministry requires funding. Upon checking the records, I have discovered that you are * Amount behind on pledge * behind

on your monthly pledge of * Amount of
pledge *. The church community would appre-
ciate it if you could bring the contributions on
your pledge up-to-date as soon as possible. If
there is some reason that you cannot keep your
pledge up-to-date, please let me know so that
your pledge can be adjusted to suit your
circumstances.

Sincerely yours,

Obviously, the above examples are limited in scope
and are not intended to cover all aspects of church
member financial giving. There are many circumstances in which such letters might or might not be
used depending upon individual family situations.
However, these examples should give you some ideas
of the many ways document generation can be used in
your ministry.

System comments

Document generation is generally accomplished
using word processing software that can access the
data base and spreadsheet files. Thus, an integrated
package with data base, spreadsheet, and word
processing functions is required to achieve effective
document generation.

Your word processing software may be able to
interface with some customized software. In other
words, files that have been created from customized
software may be accessible through the document
generation portions of your word processing software.
However, data files that have been created through
customized software may not readily work (integrate)
with word processing. This should be carefully
examined in order to reduce unexpected surprises.

For your system to save time, planning is necessary when using document generation. Give careful thought to the ways this technique can be used, or more work will be created rather than reduced. In addition, accuracy is important because the computer will be producing so many documents that it is impractical to proofread every piece. Thus, your data base must contain accurate data if selected items are to be inserted into the body of a letter or other document.

Document generation should not be used if a particular document does not contain any inserted information from the data base. The document is simply printed. In addition, if you need twenty copies of some report, print one copy and duplicate the other nineteen on a copy machine. It is usually more costly to print twenty copies on your computer printer as compared to using a copy machine. Of course, if a duplicating machine is not available, then your only alternative is to print all copies on the computer printer.

Primary Software (Required):
Word processing
Data base
Document generator, usually an optional part of the
  word processing software that must be purchased
  in addition to the basic software.
Secondary Software (Optional):
Customized

Pastoral Records

General comments

The organization and maintenance of pastoral records is a large administrative area. These records present a history of a pastor's ministry, which are important in tracing the histories of churches and church members. Pastoral records include many items, for example, a chronological listing of all baptisms completed, marriages performed, church members received, funerals performed. Such records are vital for a pastor to maintain as his or her ministry grows and changes.

Several manual ways exist for the maintenance of pastoral records. Several well-known religious bookstores and denominational publishing houses sell specially organized journals for pastoral records. Some pastors also create a manual recording system to meet specific needs. While manual systems are good, they are more time-consuming than automated systems.

A computer can organize and keep pastoral records very easily. Then reports and records can be printed as needed. Such an application can save time in the administrivia of modern day ministry.

Suggested data to be maintained

Listing of pastorates served including dates, church name, address, membership, salary, etc.

Baptisms performed including name of person baptized, address, place of baptism, age, date of baptism, date of birth, etc.

New church members received or confirmed including name of new member, address, date received, marital status, age, how received (profession, transfer, confirmation).

Marriages performed including names of couple, addresses before and after marriage, date of marriage, ages, occupations, location of ceremony.

Funerals performed including name of deceased, address, date of funeral, date of death, age at death, reason for death, church membership status, location of funeral.

Chronological listing of sermons delivered including sermons title, scriptural text, date delivered, location delivered, etc. (See chapter 11 for a more detailed discussion of sermon records.)

Other records of importance such as:

Special meetings held, e.g., evangelistic, social activism, etc.

Special funds raised for special purposes

New church buildings, parsonages, or additions built

Lectures and/or special addresses delivered

Writings published

Personal giving

Salary and benefits received

Special personal gifts received

Vacations taken

Possible reports and other output documents

The type of reports printed will depend upon a pastor's specific needs and desires. You may wish to print reports on a periodic basis and then place the output in a three-ring notebook as a continuous record of pastoral information.

Flexibility in the formats of reports is essential in order to meet your needs. Thus, report generating software will be necessary in this application. Also, you should be careful not to waste paper in this application because the tendency may exist to print too much information, which is not useful for your daily ministry.

Some word processing documents can also be created through document generation then interfaced with the pastoral records data base. For example, this process may be helpful when you are asked to verify the baptism of a person in a church you served twenty years ago.

Systems comments

Interface with the membership data base could be useful in certain instances. For example, when a new member is entered into the membership data base, the pastoral record is updated automatically. These automatic entries could also happen for baptisms and deaths that are recorded in the membership data base. Such an interface will reduce duplication of effort because the data does not have to be entered more than once.

Primary Software (Required):
Data base
Report generator
Secondary Software (Optional):
Word processing
Customized

Name and Address Lists

General comments

It is often important for a pastor to develop and maintain a variety of name and address lists for many purposes. These lists can be used for mailings to specified committees, selected age groups, sending the annual Christmas letter or card, alerting community leaders to an emerging problem, and many other special needs. (This application overlaps with other applications that have been previously discussed; however, name and address lists also have certain unique characteristics that require some consideration.)

A manual system used to keep name and address lists can be used, but such a system is time-consuming. Manually maintained lists are found on paper, copier labels, carbon labels, and other common media forms that require periodic retyping. A computer eliminates duplication of effort by maintaining the lists in a common data base. Using query functions and other data base features, selected name and address lists can be generated easily.

Suggested data to be maintained

The data to be maintained in this application includes all information previously listed in the membership data base application (chapter 9). In addition to the data suggested previously, a code can be developed to help identify certain groups. The code eliminates duplication of effort where a person is listed on more than one list. Thus, you need to enter the name and address once followed by all code designations for that person.

The code can take any form that you desire. The following is an example of one particular form:

1A = Chairperson, Church Board
2A = Member, Church Board
2C = Member, Education Committee
3F = Member, Finance Committee

Then, in your file you may have:

Ms. Ellen Honesty
123 Integrity Lane
Central City, USA 99999

Codes: 1A, 2A, 3F

Mr. John Forthright
2175 Loud Thunder Road
Central City, USA 99999

Codes: 2A, 2C, 3F

The code system shown above is a simple example of what is possible. If you wish to use names and address lists effectively in a computer, you need to invent a code system that meets your needs. Some software will include a name and address code system, and other software will not.

Possible reports and other output documents

Reports in this application basically consist of lists that would print on the printer or display on the screen in various forms. These might include:

1. A work list on regular computer paper to use for updating or other purposes.
2. Labels for mailing purposes. There are many types of labels including self-adhesive, gummed, chesire, etc. In addition, labels can come in 1-across, 2-across, and 4-across types. The 4-across labels are the least expensive per label, allowing you to print four labels on each print line. (The word *across* is often replaced with *up*, although *across* is much more definitive of how such labels work. For example, 1-across would be 1-up, 2-across would be 2-up, and 4-across would be 4-up.)
3. Insertion into word processing documents. This was previously discussed in the "Mass Mailings and Repetitive Reports" section of this chapter.

A more concrete example of a report is when a meeting notice needs to be sent to all members of the church's finance committee. Using the code designations described above, the computer is told to print a set of 1-up labels for the code designation 3F. The result is a label list of all finance comittee members on 1-up labels. In like manner, if you wanted to send a mailing to members of the education committee, then you would choose 2C. If you wanted to send a mailing to both finance *and* education committee members for a joint meeting, then you would choose 2C and 3F. Of course, to send the monthly newsletter to all persons on your mailing list, the computer is told to print all names and addresses in the file on the appropriate labels.

List and label reports will probably require a report generator unless you have specific software to print what is needed.

System comments

The membership data base application is the key to effective use of name and address lists. You will initially load the name and address information through the membership data base system. The data base sorting routines will then produce the necessary sorts, e.g., 2A or 3F, and place the information into a print file. Thus, make sure your data base package has an adequate sorting facility.

Primary Software (Required):
Data base
Report generator
Sort routines, if not part of data-base software
Secondary Software (Optional):
Word processing, if you need document generation
Customized

Newsletter Processing and Production

General comments

Every church is in the business of communication—communication about Jesus Christ and his message. This communication occurs in various ways, depending upon the needs of the church and the surrounding community. The modes of communication include preaching, study groups, church school classes, fellowship groups, the Sunday bulletin, and many other forms. However, one of the most common modes of modern church communication is the newsletter.

The church newsletter comes in many forms, from very simple single sheets to lengthy epistles. Yet the one common thread among almost all newsletters is *church news*. The news covers many events, from the birth of a church member's grandchild to anniversary listings to the planning meeting for the big bazaar to the church board minutes. In addition to the news are the religious filler items such as jokes, poems, and other stories. In any case, the news is important to church life, and the newsletter is the medium by which church news is distributed and communicated on a consistent basis.

Many churches publish the newsletter on a monthly basis, while others send a newsletter each week. This varies depending upon the churches' needs. Some of the information in the newsletter (such as titles and headings) remain static while other information changes. Changeable information includes the monthly or weekly calendar and news events. Most of the information (95 percent) must be edited each time the newsletter is published.

In many smaller churches, the pastor is often the editor who directs every phase of newsletter production from gathering the news to running the mimeograph machine. Being the reporter, managing editor, editor-in-chief, and publisher requires much time and effort. Even if the pastor is not responsible for all phases of newsletter production, he or she must generally oversee mailing deadlines, publication details, and often submits stories and devotional items to be included in the newsletter.

The computer can help a pastor enormously in newsletter production, and is particularly useful if he or she is responsible for all phases of the production process. The "cut and paste" of editorial work is eliminated, and the editorial process is substantially simplified. In fact, the computer could reduce the amount of time needed for newsletter production by 30 percent to 60 percent, depending upon the church and its needs.

Suggested data to be maintained

News file to record notes for next newsletter printing:

> Sources of information
> People involved
> Dates, if applicable
> Event, if a meeting, dinner, etc.
> Brief description of news story
> Other comments

Filler file to contain anecdotes, etc.

> Source of item (needed for credit purposes)
> Type, e.g., joke, poem
> Date used
> Actual text of item or file where item can be located

Both the news and filler files can use word processing and/or data base software. A textual description using word processing software that incorporates the data above may be sufficient, or a data base list may be more efficient, depending upon your needs.

Possible reports and other output documents

Before actually composing the newsletter, the reminder news file can be printed. Then, you would choose the items to be included in the next newsletter. These items are then transferred to an active editing file to create the newsletter, and at the same time they are deleted from the news file so that only unused items remain.

Another report to be printed is all filler items that have a blank field in the date section. In other words, you print only those filler items that you have not used previously. Choose the filler items you want, and move them to your active editing file. At the same time, the item should be marked in the filler file with the newsletter date for future reference so it is not used again.

A third report is the actual newsletter in either draft form for editing purposes or in final form ready to be duplicated. However, the final form should be printed on a letter quality printer if you are going to cut a stencil for duplication purposes.

System comments

Word processing is used almost exclusively for this application. Also, remember to update the news and filler files as each newsletter is produced. If those files are not updated, time will be wasted during the production process because you will be printing and reading material that was used in previous newsletters.

Primary Software (Required):
Word processing
Secondary Software (Optional):
Data base, if your needs demand it

Interests, Talents, and Skills Inventory

General comments

Finding persons to fill committee positions and other lay leadership roles in the church can be a complex task. Quite often, the pastor becomes the "gopher" in trying to find people willing to work in the variety of tasks needed in the church. In other words, the pastor must "go for" him and "go for" her, attempting to convince them of the valuable contribution they can make in a particular position. This task can be a frustrating, time-consuming, thankless, but necessary job that frequently results in asking the same persons over and over again to do a job because you know they'll do it.

The tedium of this task is often rooted in the lack of adequate information about church members' abilities and interests. Retrieving information for filling church positions is where the computer can help. The maintenance of church members' talents and skills can enable you to easily identify persons with the needed expertise to fill specified positions. For example, the computer can print a list of persons who are or have been professional teachers, as you search for potential church school teachers. On the other hand, through an interest inventory, you could also print a list of persons who have expressed an interest in teaching church school, even if they lack professional education credentials. If the interests, talents, and skills of church members are in the computer system, your creativity is the only limit in finding the right person to assume a job that suits his or her interests and abilities.

Suggested data to be maintained

Name of church member
Address and telephone number
Age
Occupation and Employer (Occupations should be classified into general categories, e.g., banker, high school teacher, farmer
Education

Professional or vocational level attributes, i.e., due to job

Interests, e.g., music

Talents, e.g., plays organ, trumpet, piano

Skills, e.g., specializes in organ

Avocational level attributes, i.e., due to hobbies, etc.

Interests, e.g., electronics, woodworking

Talents, e.g., amateur radio operator

Skills, e.g., good teacher, carpentry

Service history. The service history of the person lists his or her past membership and leadership responsibilities by date in the church. This data helps you avoid asking the same people over and over again to do the same job. (Service history was previously discussed in the "Membership Data Base" section of chapter 9.)

Many other possible data items could be maintained in this application depending upon your particular needs. Many denominations and their publishing houses have suggested interest, talent, and skill inventories used to gather data for the church. You may wish to obtain one or more of these inventories and use them as a guide for the kinds of data you might keep in the computer.

Possible reports and other output documents

Reports will be printed on the printer or displayed on the screen based upon your specific needs. You would tell the computer to produce a list for you that contains the names, addresses, telephone numbers, and service history of all persons with a particular skill or interest. For example, suppose you need to find three new members for the finance committee. The computer could print a list of all church members with formal training, experience, or interest in finance. Headings for this report might be:

Name	Address	Telephone Number	Vocational I. T. or S	Avocational I. T. or S	Service History	Accept?

The acceptance column is for you to make handwritten notes, indicating acceptance or rejection of the position, or other relevant comments.

Because you will need reports in this application to meet specific requirements, a report generator is necessary. This will provide the needed flexibility in organizing the reports to fit your specific requirements.

System comments

Careful thought and planning should be given to the organization of this application because it can interface with many other data base files. Obviously, it links with the membership data base in many ways and could even be a subset of the membership data base. In addition, this application can link with the service history of church members to avoid the pitfalls of asking the same people to do the same jobs again. Thus, you should carefully analyze the organization of this data and use an automated interest, talents, and skills inventory to save duplication of effort in your overall information systems controls.

Primary Software (Required):
   Data base
   Report generator
Secondary Software (Optional):
   None

Church Financial Planning

General comments

One of the pastor's major responsibilities is to be constantly aware of the church's financial status. Obviously, such knowledge must be close at hand for accurate and complete planning for the church's program. The pastor is often called upon to provide information about the relationship between membership and stewardship, and to share in the formulation of chuch budgets. A pastor may also be asked "what-if" questions about the church budget and possible resulting ministry programs.

Calculations involving budgets and what-if projections can be complex, due to changing parameters and, therefore, exceedingly time-consuming when using paper, pencil, and a hand calculator. A computer, however, can take hours of hand calculations and complete them in seconds. Spreadsheet software can be used to make what-if projections and construct budget scenarios from data already available in your membership statistics and current budget. Such projections coupled with program planning helps you to know what areas of church ministry can be emphasized and what monetary realities can be expected.

Suggested data to be maintained

Number of church members
Per capita giving
Current year budget figures
Current year actual receipts
Pledges to actual income ratio, e.g., 91 percent of
   total pledges have been received year-to-date or
   in the current month.

Possible reports and other output documents

From the data items suggested above, a variety of budget projections and planning information can be obtained. This information needs to be reported in a way that is meaningful to you and the church. You can use the spreadsheet software printing capabilities to produce the reports you need.

A regular report generator may not be very useful here. Report generators are usually associated with data base software and may be limited and possibly useless with your spreadsheet software. This restriction depends entirely upon your software package and the level of integration achieved between the data base and spreadsheet functions. If an integrated software package with the data base and spreadsheet functions is not available and your spreadsheet software has a simple report generator, then some reports can be produced according to your specifications.

System comments

Some spreadsheet software can read information from existing data files. If your software has this capability, then it should be used with large data files. Such a function will save large blocks of time in the overall system operation because the data does not have to be entered a second time. On the other hand, if the data from existing data files is relatively small, then it is probably more efficient to re-key this information. Common sense is needed in determining whether data should be automatically read by the software or re-keyed.

Once a budget has been completed and printed on paper, a tendency exists to rely too heavily upon it. It is easy to believe that if the computer printed all those numbers, then it must be the gospel truth. However, don't believe everything you read. There is no magic in computer projections. Remember that financial planning projections are only as reliable as the numbers upon which they are based. There is a margin of error when considering projections, and your overall system must have enough flexibility to accommodate such error. In addition, disasters do occur in a church's life, which drastically change a church's financial picture requiring new projections. Thus, the planning projections produced from a pastoral computer should be taken with a grain of salt. Your overall system will be more effective if the computer projections are tempered with common sense and reality.

Primary Software (Required):
 Spreadsheet
Secondary Software (Optional):
 Data base
 Report generator
 Customized

Personal Finance

General comments

 The world of personal finance can be a complicated, often depressing adventure. The constant battle to make ends meet is frustrating and anxiety laden, especially on the frequently meager salary of a local church pastor. Almost all seminaries and Bible schools that train pastors do not provide any classes on personal finance management and explanations of tax laws that pertain to the pastor's situation. Yet, when entering your first pastoral appointment, the reality of monthly expenses and unusual tax regulations strike. For example, the United States Internal Revenue

Service (IRS) considers pastors in somewhat of a unique category. Because of current laws, the IRS defines pastors as self-employed persons for Social Security purposes. On the other hand, the self-employed status is not necessarily assured for income tax status. In addition, pastors who are citizens of the United States must have their church or employing body declare a housing allowance, an unusual tax-exempt portion of income that follows special rules. In general, the lack of training plus unclear tax laws that apply to pastors leads to confusion and feelings of being victimized by the system.

In spite of the personal financial pressure you may feel as a pastor, a responsible attitude with finance serves as a model for your congregation. While your parishioners may not know your exact personal financial condition, they will have a general understanding and knowledge of how well your personal finances are handled. Even if you are confused about personal finance, your computer can help organize data in the following areas:

—Monthly budget, primarily for planning purposes
—Checkbook, showing current balances, completing reconciliations, and possibly even automatic checkwriting
—Tax information
—Other financial concerns, e.g., investment.

How extensively a computer is used in your personal finances depends greatly upon your needs. For example, if you write less than ten checks each month, then a computer is probably not needed in maintaining your checkbook. On the other hand, if you write one hundred checks per month, the computer is needed to save time.

Regardless of your income level and checkbook needs, the computer should be used to assist with tax records. Tax data that is summarized by a computer at the end of a year can save immense amounts of time for you or the person who prepares your tax return. Particularly if you employ a professional tax preparer who charges by the hour, direct savings can be achieved. This savings results from the reduction of the number of hours needed to complete the return through summarized tax data available from the computer.

Please note that I am NOT a lawyer, tax accountant, or financial advisor. While I can suggest ways in which you can use a computer in your personal finances, I am not qualified to give you specific advice on taxes and personal finance. Thus, I suggest you consult a lawyer or tax adviser to get more specific information about the laws and rules that pertain to your individual situation.

Suggested data to be maintained

Monthly budget:

Income—
  Salary
  Honorariums
  Personal Gifts
  Miscellaneous
Expenses—
  Tithe and charitable contributions
  Mortgage or rent if not living in a church-owned residence
  Utilities, including electricity, gas, telephone, water, sewer, etc.
  Loan payments
  Insurance premiums
  Credit card payments
  Newspaper, magazines, books

Entertainment
Automobile expenses
Household expenses, including food (other than utilities)
Savings account deposit
Miscellaneous

Checkbook:
Checking account deposits
Current account balance
For each check
Check number
Amount
Date
Payee
Special codes for personal reference, e.g., UT meaning utilities

Tax information (can be drawn from budget and/or checkbook):
For the United States
Housing allowance
Utility expenses
Other housing expenses
Schedule A, Form 1040 deductions
Medical
Taxes
Interest
Contributions
Casualty and theft losses
Miscellaneous
Schedule C, Form 1040 (self-employed)
Income, using special rules that apply to clergy Expenses (see a 1040 Schedule C)
For countries other than the United States, consult the appropriate tax rules for creating tax data files and lists.

Possible reports and other output documents

Reports can be generated in three categories to match the areas listed in the previous section:

1. Monthly budget report. This report is used to help maintain budget expenses. It should include a section that shows projected or actual income versus projected or actual expenses. From this report, you should be able to determine if sufficient income is available to meet expenses.

2. Checking account report. This report can show the current checking account balance after all expenses are paid. In addition, it can list all outstanding checks and have a check reconciliation routine to assist with that monthly chore.

3. Tax information report. This report can be generated whenever you have need for it. It will be primarily used at the end of each tax year in preparing a tax return. It should include all relevent items for tax return preparation including totals, e.g., the grand total paid on all utilities, grand total paid on all interest, etc.

A report generator for the above suggested reports would probably be advantageous. You may wish to generate the reports in a variety of ways, depending upon your particular monthly or yearly needs. A report generator is needed for such flexibility.

System comments

This application will take substantial work to organize and maintain through the computer. Creation of personal financial data on your computer requires careful analysis of the data that is important for you.

There is no need to interface this application with others discussed in this book because it is entirely personal finance. A spreadsheet package integrated with customized software would probably be the best software option for an efficient system.

Primary Software (Required):
  Spreadsheet
  Customized, if available
  Report generator
Secondary Software (Optional):
  Customized

Tickler Files

General comments

A tickler file is a place where notes about a particular subject related to a certain date can be stored and retrieved. In other words, tickler files are vehicles to help you remember things to be done on certain dates.

Almost all pastors have large amounts of information to remember. In addition, much of this information is detailed and often complex. Most pastors use a mental system of tickler files to save information and details in order to avoid writing it on a piece of paper. However, as almost every human being has experienced, mental notes are not as easily remembered as we usually expect them to be. Also, mental notes are often confused with one another, resulting in a strange mixture of details that don't make sense.

Other pastors use written tickler files on index cards, scraps of paper, napkins, the backs of envelopes, and other materials. Written systems, while generally better than the mental kind, can be hard to assimilate and time-consuming to keep.

Tickler files can be easily organized and maintained in a computer. The computer can keep tickler files by date, time, topic, or any other classification you may require. Here are some examples of tickler files:

Date: June 23
Topic: Finance committee
Notes:
—Committee meeting at 7:30 P.M. on June 25.
—Finalize agenda. Agenda should include discussion of anonymous undesignated gift.
—Plan missions budget for next year.
—Call committee chairperson to discuss last minute details.

Date: August 28
Topic: September Newsletter, items to include
Notes:
—Mr. & Mrs. John Jenkins had a baby daughter on August 9. Baby's name: Nicole Ann.
—Fall bazaar on Oct. 23. Committee meets on Sept. 19, 8:00 P.M.

Date: Sept. 12
Topic: Estimated tax payment
Notes:
—Get Sept. 15 estimated tax payment ready!!
—Mail payment on the 14th.

Tickler files in the computer illustrated by the above examples are a method of remembering. They are easy to enter and maintain, and yet are invaluable for planning purposes and other needs.

Suggested data to be maintained

Date, either in a specific or general format, e.g., February 6 or March notes.

Time, if appropriate. This can also be imbedded in the notes section depending upon your needs.

Topic, e.g., committee, newsletter, Sunday announcements, personal.

Notes. Notes should be succinct, concise, and easily readable. Avoid long sentences.

Possible reports and other output documents

Reports can be generated in one of two formats.

1. By date. A particular date or range of dates can be printed or displayed. The tickler files can also be sorted alphabetically by topic within the date or dates selected.

2. By topic. Tickler files in the computer that pertain to one subject can be printed or displayed. For example, a report could be printed of all tickler files with a topic of "newsletter." If desired, the report could be sorted by date within each topic.

The methods by which reports generate are limited by the software being used for tickler files. If data base management software is used, then a report generator is needed. On the other hand, if word processing software is used for this application, then the print routines in the word processing package will control report generation. Also, remember that reports may either print on the printer or be displayed on the screen.

System comments

Interfacing with other applications is probably not necessary in the tickler file application. However, some interfacing may be helpful. For example, when you record the death of a church member in the membership data base, the software could be programmed to automatically create a tickler file with a date one year in the future as a reminder to call on the family. (See "Ministry to the Bereaved" in chapter 9.)

Tickler files should be planned to follow your work patterns and particular needs. By following existing work patterns, your overall information system will become more efficient. Thus, careful thought should be given to the organization of this application that optimal benefits are produced for you.

Primary Software (Required):
Data base

    OR

Word processing
Secondary Software (Optional):
Customized

Judicatory Reports

General comments

More pastors of mainline denominations are required to submit regular and periodic reports to parent judicatory bodies. Much of the required report data can already be found in membership and pastoral records data bases. For example, the number of baptisms, new members, and other information is already in those data bases. The computer can summarize the data in a way that follows the judicatory reports and then print it using the report generator.

I cannot presume to list every possible judicatory report from every denomination. Such a list would cover literally thousands of pages and would definitely be very dull reading! The key in using the computer for judicatory reports is based upon the reporting needs AND in using data that already exists in your data bases. Using pre-existing data saves enormous amounts of time in generating the reports.

If the data is already in the computer, then you must decide if judicatory reporting should be done on your computer. For example, if you are required to complete a certain report only once each year and it has just ten statistical entries, which cannot be summarized from existing data, then the form should be completed using paper, pencil, and calculator. The question to ask is if using the computer for a certain report is worth the effort expended on the machine. If it isn't, then don't do the report on the computer just because you have a computer.

Suggested data to be maintained

The data to be kept for judicatory reports is specific to your reporting requirements. As mentioned previously, the membership and pastoral records data bases probably have the information needed for most reports.

Possible reports and other output documents

The report generated will obviously be specific to your judicatory requirements, using the report generator to produce the needed information. Then simply transfer the information to the report form by hand.

Some denominations may offer their report forms with either pin feed or tractor feed mechanisms. If this is so, then the forms can be placed in the printer and the report printed directly onto them. However, direct printing on denominationally supplied computer forms will probably require customized software to line up columns and rows.

System comments

Major integration with the membership and pastoral records data bases is required in this application. In fact, if the data is already there, this application is completed with ONLY those two data bases and the report generator. Calculation of the necessary totals will probably require a spreadsheet or customized software. Thus, the data base, spreadsheet, and report generator software must be integrated to complete this application. If such integration is not possible with your software, then customized software is required for this application.

Primary Software (Required):
  Data base
  Report generator
  Spreadsheet (to calculate totals)
Secondary Software (Optional):
  Customized

SECTION 4

IN CONCLUSION

13

Computer Cautions

Finally . . . think about these things.

Philippians 4:8

It is no secret that computers are excessively glamorized. Articles, books, advertisements, speeches, and other sources constantly bombard the average person with the flash and dash of computers. An inexperienced person who purchases a computer is often led to believe that the machine runs itself and will solve all his or her problems. Still others believe that computers are the ultimate devices that will free humanity from the mundane tasks of living.

Unfortunately, these beliefs are built on myths created by vendors and hobbyists who don't understand computers. Computer professionals know that all is not as it appears in the computer world. Computers never quite work in the ways most inexperienced people expect or assume. Whether a multimillion dollar super-computer or a small micro-computer is being purchased, there are many cautions to consider. Using a personal computer in pastoral ministry requires thoughtful reflection upon these cautions, or you may find your time excessively consumed by the computer, which will result in a less effective ministry.

None of these cautions should detract or discourage you from using a computer in ministry; however, they should be considered thoughtfully in the light of your ministry. Indeed, the cautions should be considered in view of the impact a computer may have upon your own life and the resulting implications for your ministry. Thus, review the computer cautions, and place them in a balance between the creative and destructive forces that enable or disable the effective utilization of a computer in pastoral ministry.

Confidentiality of Information

One of the key applications of a computer in pastoral ministry is a church membership data base. Some of the information kept in a membership data base is confidential.

Every pastor is deeply aware of the confidential trust he or she must maintain in the pastor/parishioner relationship. This trust must also logically extend beyond the pastor to include the tools of pastoral ministry. For example, file folders should be locked in a filing cabinet with access restricted to the pastor. Thus, the following questions are appropriate for a pastor who uses a computer in pastoral ministry.

—How will confidential information maintained through the computer be protected?

—What steps and safeguards should be taken to prevent access of the information by unauthorized persons?

—Is locking floppy disks in a filing cabinet or a small personal safe a sufficient safeguard?

—What security software is available for your computer to help protect confidential information? Does the data base, word processing, spreadsheet, or customized software have any security features?

—Will church members believe that their privacy is being invaded by using a computer? If so, what can be done to lessen their fears?

—Will church members feel that they are simply a number in your ministry rather than persons who have real human needs?

Compatibility

If the church owns a computer, compatibility with the pastoral computer is probably desirable. Full compatibility will save duplication of effort in name and address changes, entry of new member information, and other important areas. (Compatibility means that a complete software and data exchange is possible between two different computers without using any special communications or conversion software.)

Compatibility is a buzz word in the computer world that sounds impressive but says little. Many vendors claim compatibility between different computers but, in fact, such compatibility is often sorely lacking.

In essence, compatibility is a matter of degrees. Some computers are more compatible than others. Compatibility involves many factors including:

—Software
—Data storage
—Disk formatting
—Communications

If a church already has a computer, the perfect situation for the pastor is to have exactly the same kind of computer as the church's computer, but this may not be practical. The next-to-ideal situation would be where data required by both the church and pastoral computer could be simply and easily transferred between the two machines. In other words, if you have an ABC computer and the church has an XYZ computer, can data be transferred exactly as it exists between the two machines without requiring additional hardware and software?

Only vendors can ultimately answer the compatibility question; however, they often don't know the answers, either. Thus, considerable research may be required on your part to discover compatibility levels.

Initial Data Entry

Initial data entry can be a time-consuming task after the computer is installed. The initial entry can be accomplished by you, the church secretary, a volunteer, a spouse, or a temporary employee that is specifically hired for data entry. Examples of initial data entry include:

—A church of 300 individual members with 25 unique data items for each member will total 7,500 individual data entries into the computer!

—To maintain sermons previously preached in the computer, each one will have to be typed into the computer.

Initial data entry is an important consideration in the purchase of a computer. The data must be entered, and you will have to decide who, when, what, how, and how long when thinking about initial data entry.

Backups

Backups are another area to consider in planning for a pastoral computer. Backups are electronic copies of all the information maintained on your disks. A backup disk is a copy of a regular disk, much like a piece of paper is copied on a copy machine.

Backups are vital in the operation of a pastoral ministry computer. Backups are important in case a disk becomes damaged, data is accidentally erased, the computer burns in a fire, or another disaster occurs. As you become more dependent upon the computer for pastoral ministry, backups should be executed for all changed information on a daily basis. In addition, it may be wise to complete a second backup each week and place it in a secure location, such as a safety deposit box at the bank or a personal safe in your home away from the church. Off-site backup storage provides protection should a fire destroy the computer, the machine is stolen, it becomes wet from water leaking through the roof, or any other disastrous situation. If you have a backup stored in a secure location, another computer compatible with your data can be secured relatively quickly, which allows you to continue computer operations. Backups are vital in the operation of a pastoral ministry computer.

The Validity of Electronic Information

Almost all pastors have had former church members write and ask for an official verification of baptism, membership transfer, confirmation, profession of faith, and/or other common, but important dates. These dates serve many purposes such as Social Security benefits verification upon retirement, membership information for a new church, or genealogy needs.

Verification data for important church member data frequently comes directly out of the pastor's personal records. That information is found other times in the church's historical records. Information of this sort usually consists of manually maintained handwritten records that serve as legal verification for either church or government bodies.

Several legal questions surrounding computers have developed as their use becomes more prevalent.

These questions relate primarily to the validity of electronically maintained information.

It is important for pastors to be aware of the developing legal issues about the validity of electronically stored information. For example, suppose your records for baptisms are electronically maintained through a computer. At some point, the machine may be used to verify a baptism for the Social Security date of birth requirements in the United States. It is within the realm of possibility that the Social Security Administration may question the validity of the data you have provided, if they discover the computer was used in the verification.

At the present time, no clear precedents have been established in either denominational church courts or most government courts regarding the validity and value of electronically recorded information. Thus, until the questions are answered more clearly, a pastor should use caution in maintaining *only* electronic data for important records such as baptisms. It may be wise, for example, to generate printed copies of each baptism and place them in a three ring notebook. Maintenance of both printed and electronic records would probably be more acceptable to officials who require printed evidence.

It is true that the validity of information question for a pastor with a computer is not a great threat and probably poses very little danger for your ministry. However, this problem doubtless will grow more ominous as society becomes more dependent upon computers. Thus, an awareness of the growing questions about the validity of electronically stored information will help you to make appropriate plans, if necessary.

The Computer as an Excuse

It is easy to let the computer become an excuse for not working or completely discharging pastoral responsibilities. For example, it seems that most pastors do not relish the thought of home visitation or calling. As a result, pastors use a variety of excuses in order to be relieved of that often tedious responsibility. One frequently used excuse is administrative work. Letters, reports, filing, typing, and other administrivia keep pastors from their calling duties. In other words, pastors often LET administrative work prevent them from calling and completing other types of work they may not enjoy.

The computer is meant to reduce the administrivia of the pastoral load—not increase it. Yet, in the future it may become easy for a pastor to say that he or she is too busy to do certain things because "Something's wrong with the computer and I have to fix it," or "It's the computer's fault," or "I'm working with the computer." In a society where the great majority of people do not understand the computer's capabilities nor where computer demythologizing has not occurred, working with the machine could easily become a convenient excuse and simple method for a pastor not to do his or her work. Such an excuse is a direct contradiction of a tool meant to reduce the administrative, organizational load, rather than increase it.

When a pastoral computer is first installed, you must learn how to use it. This results in additional time to begin using a computer in ministry. However, at some point, you should become familiar enough with the machine to make practical use of it, requiring less time. Therefore, be aware of the computer's impact so that it does not become an excuse for ignoring the real work of pastoral ministry.

Computer Widows, Widowers, and Orphans

In some instances, when a person's hobby or work becomes so important, he or she often ignores spouse, family, and friends. One example of this problem is the sports' widow (or widower), which is a common malady that appears on World Series days or on Super Bowl Sunday in the United States. Professional counselors have verified that extramarital affairs occur not only with other human beings, but also with jobs and hobbies.

The widow, widower, or orphan syndrome may also develop within a family that has a computer. It has been documented that in some families with a computer, this syndrome has occurred. Whether male or female, some spouses have become so intrigued by the computer that it seems their nonstop communication is limited to bits and bytes, RAM and ROM, floppy and hard disks, MS-DOS and C/PM, and all the other computer terms.

This syndrome is not a new theme or trend in our society. Hobby or job widows, widowers, and orphans have existed for decades, but the problem seems accentuated by the recent explosion of home computers. If a spouse is so deeply interested in computers, then logically, the other spouse will be ignored in favor of the machine. The person who is involved with computers will begin talking at the spouse about computers rather than dealing with the emotional needs of the marital relationship.

A pastor's time is generally pressured enough with the demanding activities required of him or her in order to maintain the church. As a result, family and friends are often ignored. If the computer is not kept within its context as a tool, a pastor will end up having a computer affair. Being aware of this potential hazard, you should consciously and intentionally make sure that the computer helps you with your pastoral administrivia thereby giving you extra time for additional pastoral work and additional precious moments with your spouse, family, and friends. Therefore, whether single or married, pastors should be on guard that computer infatuation does not jeopardize personal relationships.

Common Sense

When using a computer, a common temptation exists to put everything into a computer and do every task through the machine. This temptation is self-defeating because some tasks and information do not work well in a computer. Such tasks take more time and cost more money when compared to a manual system.

Common sense should be used when using a pastoral computer system. For example, if you have to address only one envelope, use a pen, pencil, or typewriter rather than printing only one label from the computer. It is simpler, easier, and less time-consuming to address one envelope by hand.

Each information management task should be considered in light of its appropriateness for a computer. Common sense will guide you in making these decisions and should be used liberally with a pastoral computer system.

No Quick Miracles

Don't expect a miracle overnight. The computer is a tool and it should be respected as such. It may take one, two, three, four, or even five to ten years to make a computer fully functional in your pastoral ministry. Don't let computer advertisements or the vendor deceive you with the myth that all you have to do is bring it home, plug it in, turn it on, and the rest is magic. You have to do the work. You have to push the buttons. The computer is a useless, inanimate object that has no value for ministry unless someone tells it what to do and when to do it.

I am often asked by individuals what is the one piece of advice in twenty-five words or less that I can give about computers. I always tell them, "Expect the unexpected." Expect the unexpected. Even in large corporations who employ computer professionals that have used computers for twenty-five years and who carefully plan, analyze costs, and manage facilities, something unexpected always happens in the computer operation. In the pastoral ministry, no matter how much planning and analysis occurs prior to the purchase and installation of a pastoral computer, invariably something will have been missed. This could be a very simple thing such as an extra printer ribbon, a vital cable, or a telephone for communications. Any number of unexpected factors may occur that can cause a frustrating problem. Therefore, expect the unexpected when dealing with computers. Expecting the unexpected will reduce your frustration, increase your patience, and enable you to develop an efficient and effective ministry information system.

Bottom-line Responsibility

A pastor who uses a computer is responsible for the data in the machine. In other words, YOU are responsible for maintaining accurate data that reflects the integrity of your ministry. A periodic check of the data in the computer to verify its accuracy is a good information management practice. For example, it may be prudent once a year to print out all electronically maintained information about each church member. This information can then be distributed to each church member for accuracy verification. Through this method, each church member has partial ownership of the data, enabling the pastor to maintain data accuracy and integrity, and lessening a member's fear that their data is inaccurate and not easily changed if something is in error. Whether you use the method suggested above or another of your own choosing, you are ultimately responsible for the data in your computer and your overall pastoral ministry information system.

Who Is the Real Manager?

It is vitally important that the computer work for you. You should not work for the computer. People who use computers frequently relate feelings of being directed or manipulated by the machine. This directed feeling is very real and often leaves a person emotionally trapped by an inanimate machine. If you ever develop the feeling that the computer is beginning to guide your pastoral ministry, telling you what to do, or negatively redefining you as a shepherd, then the machine *is* beginning to direct you. You have fallen into the trap of working for the computer, and ultimately, your ministry suffers because it is computer-managed.

As a pastor, you are the manager of your ministry. You are a vicar of Christ, a Christian shepherd who takes your guidance and grace from the one who died on the cross. The computer is merely a modern tool that helps you to be a more effective pastor by bringing Christ to the world and the world to Christ.

The Final Analysis

When purchasing a microwave oven, television set, or automobile, the buyer is responsible for making it work for his or her particular needs. This is also true of a computer. A personal computer is just that—personal. If you buy a personal computer it belongs to you. It is your machine, and you personally must make it work. Owning and operating a personal computer is a privilege that demands a responsible attitude and professional approach. A personal computer in pastoral ministry is not a hobby. It is a tool. It is a tool that can do most of the mundane administrivia tasks to help your ministry become more effective.

Epilogue: A Final Word

Go therefore and make disciples of all nations, baptizing them in the name of the Father and of the Son and of the Holy Spirit, teaching them to observe all that I have commanded you.

Matthew 28:19-20a

The Gospel according to Saint Matthew reaches its conclusion with Jesus issuing the Great Commission. The Great Commission sets forth in a few succinct words the mission and ministry of the living Body of Christ present in the world, giving the Body its discipleship directive. The universal church, regardless of denominational status, is the Body of Christ present in the world today. Each person who claims allegiance to the Body and who knows the salvation of Christ is called to labor in the vineyards of humanity through a montage of ministries that gives the Body its beauty. Thus, every member of the Body of Christ is called to faithfully minister in order to achieve the Great Commission's goal.

Within the church are certain persons exhibiting specific gifts and graces called by God to the ordained ministry. Those who choose to accept the yoke of Christ in the pastoral ministry have the unique responsibility of being both servants and leaders within the Body. There is no greater ministry in the Body than that of becoming a pastor dedicated to service and leadership. Such a task is not only a vocation or a career, but a calling of God.

Pastors are called to serve and lead within the Body. The pastor serves within the Body through caring, compassion, sensitivity, empathy, and love. The pastor leads within the Body by interpreting the Scriptures, directing worship, administering the Sacraments, and implementing missional programs.

Accurate, timely and useful information is vitally important to serving and leading in the pastoral ministry. Computers and other modern technologies are tools of information control. Properly applied, such tools are a means to the end of obeying Christ's commands carefully summarized in the Great Commission. Information tools help both pastors and the Body of Christ in processing data so that Christ is brought to the world and the world is brought to Christ.

You are called in the Spirit of the Good Shepherd to be a pastor. You are called to serve and lead in the Spirit of the Great Commission. A pastoral computer system is simply a tool for you to move forward as a disciple of Christ in the pastoral ministry and mission of his church. Whether or not you elect to use modern technological tools, my humble hope and prayer is that God will guide your service and leadership in the pastoral ministry. The grace and peace of God be with you.

Appendix 1

Brief Application Descriptions

This appendix contains brief descriptions and chapter locations of all pastoral ministry computer applications discussed in chapters 9 through 12. After most application titles are a one-word application description and the chapter number where the application is discussed.

Attendance records of Sunday worship (Pastoral; 9)—Maintenance of a church member's Sunday worship attendance records can be used to identify attendance patterns so the appropriate pastoral response can be initiated. For example, when a family who has been faithful in attendance suddenly misses three consecutive Sundays, a problem may exist suggesting the need for pastoral care.

Bereaved, ministry to the (Pastoral; 9)—The computer is used in this application to provide information about a deceased church member, his/her family, and church activities. In addition, a tickler file can be maintained to remind the pastor on the one-year anniversary of the death so that a pastoral call can be made to the spouse and/or children.

Birthday and anniversary recognition (Pastoral; 9)—On a periodic basis, the computer can print a list of church members' birthdays and anniversaries with names, addresses, telephone numbers, and other data for an appropriate pastoral response.

Bulletin preparation (Worship; 10)—A generic bulletin format is maintained in the computer's word processing system where each week the pastor or secretary can "fill in the blanks" and generate a completed bulletin either on paper or on a stencil.

Calling (Pastoral; 9)—Records are maintained in the computer about pastoral visits in the homes of parishioners or calls to the hospital.

Correspondence, general (Administrative; 12)—Letters that require editing can be completed through word processing in the computer. Standard letter paragraphs can also be stored on a computer disk so that only name, address, and salutation needs to be added to the letter. One example of a standard paragraph in a letter is a response to a request for a baptism verification from a former church member.

Counseling (Pastoral; 9)—Records and data about counselees and counseling sessions are maintained in the computer to provide a historical record of counselees and continuity in counseling sessions.

Crisis situations, ministry in (Pastoral; 9)—When a crisis occurs, the computer can generate information from the membership data base, which is helpful in making the appropriate pastoral response.

Evangelism (Pastoral; 9)—Information maintained on a computer disk about persons new to the community and on inactive church members can be used for various evangelistic emphases. For example, demographic studies in relationship to community needs can be done through the computer so that the proper evangelism program can be planned and implemented.

Financial planning for the church (Administrative; 12)—Through membership, pledge, and year-to-date giving data, spreadsheet software can be used to plan budgets and project the church's potential income.

Interests, talents and skills inventory (Administrative; 12)—Data about the interests, talents and skills of church members are maintained in the computer so persons for special jobs can be easily and simply located.

Lists, name and address (Administrative; 12)—Simple lists with names, addresses, and various codes about church activities are stored on a disk. For example, the names and addresses of education committee members can be printed on labels to send out a meeting notice.

Mass mailings and repetitive reports (Administrative; 12)—Through word processing document generation, letters with the same text can be personalized with names, addresses, and salutations of church members. Also reports and documents needed for meetings and other purposes can be repetitively generated through the computer. For example, a monthly pastor's report to the church board can be stored and retrieved from the computer as required.

Membership and confirmation training (Pastoral; 9)—Administrative details of membership and confirmation classes are maintained in the computer. This application is considered Computer Managed Instruction (CMI) rather than Computer Assisted Instruction (CAI).

Membership data base (Pastoral; 9)—A comprehensive base of information about church members. This application is the foundation of most other computer applications in the pastoral ministry.

Newsletter processing and production (Administrative; 12)—The computer is used to help write, edit, and publish the church's monthly newsletter. The computer can also be used in this application to maintain records about the newsletter issues in which filler items have been used and keep tickler files of news items to be printed in the next newsletter.

Pastoral records (Administrative; 12)—Data about a pastor's ministry including baptisms, sermons, members received, funerals, and other important information can be recorded on a disk and easily retrieved as needed.

Personal finance (Administrative; 12)—The computer can be used to maintain personal finance data for monthly budgeting, investment, checkbook, and tax purposes.

Premarital counseling (Pastoral; 9)—In this application, the computer is used to maintain data about the couple to be married and used to record the couple's responses to personality and marital inventories.

Reports (Administrative; 12)—

General—When the church requires the pastor to produce a special report, for example, on a recent evangelism emphasis, the computer can be used to help compose, edit, and print the report.

Judicatory—When a denominational body requires the

pastor to produce a report, the computer can generate the required information either through word processing or by a statistical analysis of certain information in the membership data base.

Repetitive—See "Mass mailings and repetitive reports."

Sermon (11)—

Classification—A computer can be used to help classify sermons by topic, liturgical season, Scripture, preaching date, and other relevant data.

Classification data storage—Classification data can be stored in a sermon data base so that if the pastor wants to know the titles of all sermons he or she has preached on the subject of stewardship, the computer can selectively retrieve and print such a topical list.

Illustration selection—Selection of sermon illustrations can be enhanced through a computer illustration data base. Also, when an illustration is used, the computer can record the preaching date and the title of the sermon where the illustration was used.

Outline—Producing the original sermon outline with its major points and sub-points can be completed through the computer's word processing capability.

Research on Scripture—Data from concordances, Bible dictionaries, and other reference tools can be stored in the computer for easy retrieval.

Writing, editing, and typing—The process of producing a sermon manuscript can be greatly enhanced through word processing in the computer.

Tickler files (Administrative; 12)—Tickler files are notes to remind a person to do something at a particular time. The computer can be used to record and maintain tickler file information by date and topic.

Worship resource control (Worship; 10)—Information about the physical file location, dates used, and other relevant facts about prayers, calls to worship, hymns, and other worship items can be easily stored on and retrieved from a computer disk.

Appendix 2

Glossary of Computer Terms

Architecture—The electronic and hardware design of a computer.

ASCII—American Standard Code for Information Interchange; the internal code used by all computers except IBM.

Backup—A procedure that procduces a copy of all information maintained in the computer

Baud—The speed of data transmission over a telephone line; usually used in conjunction with "modem."

Binary code (binary digits)—A code that makes use of only 0's or 1's.

Binary digit (binary code)—See "Binary code."

Bit—The smallest unit of storage in a computer; always equal to) or 1; 8 bits * 1 byte: comes from the words "*bi*nary dig*it*."

Bug—A software error.

Byte—A Unit of storage in the computer; 1 byte * 1 character; 1 byte * 8 bits in most cases.

Cathode Ray Tube (CRT, VDT, Video Display Tube)—A television monitor or terminal

Central Processing Unit (CPU)—The controlling device that provides the necessary electronic information in order that all software and hardware may achieve their specified functions.

Character—Any valid letter, number, punctuation, and or internal code used by a computer; 1 character * 1 byte.

Computer—A machine or device composed of logical electronic circuits designed to generate desired output in a specified sequence from a logical set of instructions as produced by a given set of input data.

Configuration—A description and/or diagram of the major components in a hardwae or software system.

Conversion—A procedure to change computer information in one coding scheme to another coding scheme.

Core memory—A specialized device found only in the CPU designed to store data related to the CPU's specific functions.

Cursor—The small box or line on the screen of the computer's monitor where the action occurs.

Cyberphobia—Fear of computers

Data base—A series of integrated computer files containing information relating to one or several subjects; usually data bases can be accessed by many persons and organizations.

Data Processing (DP)—The action of receiving, manipulating, and outputtin information into a specified form.

Document generation—A specialized form of word processing that allows the user to personalize mass mailings by automatically inserting name, address, salutation, and other pertinent data into the body of a standard letter or document.

Documentation—Written materials that describe hardware and/or software.

Dot matrix printer—A printer that outputs information usin pixels (dots) to form the characters; the output is not letter quality.

Double density—A method of storing data on a floppy disk; results in a greater number of characters on the disk.

Draft quality printer—A computer printer that prints documents in a form that can be easily edited; draft quality is used in producing reports, labels, and word processing document copies for editing; usually uses a dot matrix format.

Drive—A device that inputs and outputs information to and from a mass storage magnetic medium, such as a floppy or hard disk.

Dual-side floppy disk—A floppy disk with two logical sides.

EBCDIC—Extended Binary Coded Decimal Interchange Code; the internal code used by IBM computers.

EDP (Electronic Data Processing)—See "Electronic Data Processing."

Electronic Data Processing (EDP)—The action of utilizing an electronic tool to facilitate data processing.

Field—An individual data item in a record; many fields make up one record.

File—Contains information relevant to a particular subject; files are stored on disks and tapes.

Floppy disk—A mass storage magnetic media that is very fast and cost-effective.

Hardware—The physical or tangible parts of any computer that occupy space.

Input device—Provides the function of placing data and programs into the computer.

Interface—The ways and levels of efficiency in which hardware connects with other hardware and/or software links with other software.

K—Kilobyte; 1,024 bytes of storage; often shortened to 1,000 bytes of storage for simplicity.

Keypunch—A typewriter-like device used to cut holes into punched cards.

Language—A comprehensive set of signs, symbols, and commands that allows a human being to communicate with a computer, and is used by a programmer to create a computer program.

Letter quality printer—A printer that outputs information in typewriter quality.

lpm—Lines per minute; usually used when referring to printer speeds.

Machine language—A computer language in its most elementary form that represents characters through a coding scheme of only 0's and 1's.

Management Information System (MIS)—Systematized data that is both internal and external to an organization used to generate more effective and efficient administration of the organization.

Mass storage device—Stores of large amounts of data or information for instant retrieval on a magnetic medium. Examples: floppy disk drive, hard disk drive, cassette tape drive, etc.

MB (megabyte)—See "Megabyte."

Megabyte (MB)—One million bytes of storage: synonym: "Meg."

Memory—A device or devices in which information is stored.

Menu—A list of items presented on the computer's monitor from which the operator makes a choice before the program continues.

Micro-second (µs)—One one-millionth of a second, i.e., 1/1,000,000 of a second; designated by "µs".

µs (micro-second)—See "Micro-second."

MIS (Management Information System)—See "Management Information System".

Modem—A device to allow data communications over standard telephone lines. Means modulate/demodulate.

Multi-task computer—A computer capable of completing many functions simultaneously.

Multi-user computer—A computer capable of supporting many user terminals simultaneously.

Nanosecond (vs)—One one-billionth of a second, i.e., 1/1,000,000,000 of a second; designated by "vs."

vs (nanosecond)—see "Nanosecond."

Online—All data and software available to a user at any given moment without loading a different disk or tape.

Operating system—A software package that controls all internal computer functions; it is provided by the vendor.

Output device—Provides the function of retrieving data and information from a computer and displaying it in the form desired by the user.

Peripheral—A hardware device connected to a CPU that provides a specific function; examples: disk drive, terminal, etc.

Pixel—A very small mechanical or electronic dot that when used with other pixels will print characters onto paper or onto a monitor's screen; used with dot matrix printers or computer monitors.

Printer—An output device that prints information onto paper.

Program (software)—See "Software."

Programmer—A person who writes computer programs.

Programming—The art or skill of writing a program for the computer.

Prompt—A question printed on the monitor that requires an operator response before the program continues.

Protocol—A standard that allows two different computers to transfer information efficiently, i.e., a standard that permits two computers to talk with one another

Punched card—A stiff paper card with holes punched in certain patterns used to input data into a computer. This is an older technology rapidly disappearing.

Punched card reader—An input device designed to "read" punched cards.

RAM (Random Access Memory)—See "Random Access Memory."

Random Access Memory (RAM)—A computer's core memory that can be accessed by the user.

Read Only Memory (ROM)—A computer's core memory that cannot normally be accessed by the user.

Record—Contains information related to one grouping, e.g., name, address, yearly pledge, date of baptism, etc.; a "file" is composed of many records.

ROM (Read Only Memory)—See "Read Only Memory."

Single density—A method of storing data on a floppy disk; results in a smaller number of characters on the disk.

Single-side floppy disk—A floppy disk with one logical side.

Single-task computer—A computer capable of completing only one function at any given moment.

Software (program)—A logical sequence or set of instructions written in a computer language designed to achieve a specific purpose.

Software package—A set of two or more interfaced programs designed for a specific purpose.

String—A list of characters.

Terminal—An input/output device that allows communication between a human being and a computer.

Turnkey system—A combination of hardware and software usually sold at special discount prices.